"I have been a longtime proponent and practitioner of the philosophies and exercises presented by Gina Biegel and Todd Corbin. These techniques have allowed my fencers to reach numerous World Junior/Senior Championships, Pan Am Games, and four US Olympic Teams. Moreover, they prepare athletes to succeed in their lives after athletics. I strongly recommend this for all athletes, competitors, family members, coaches, and professional personnel."

—**William E. Reith**, former US Olympic fencing coach, and owner of Alcazar Fencing

"*Mindfulness for Student Athletes* is a one-of-a-kind workbook that will enable athletes of all ages, levels, and sports to take their performance to the next level. The exercises are engaging, thought-provoking, and fun. Biegel and Corbin have masterfully created exercises which build upon each other and, like a road map, guide the student athlete to tone, flex, and strengthen their mental muscles."

—**Rob Polishook, MA**, mental training coach, founder of Inside the Zone Sports Performance Group, and author of *Tennis Inside the Zone*

"This book offers student athletes simple, useable skills. Incorporating these skills into practices, competition, and daily life will allow athletes to gain and enhance their performance in every domain."

—**Amy Saltzman, MD**, author of *A Still Quiet Place for Athletes*

"Gina and Todd have created an incredible book for all who want to really learn how to apply mindfulness training to sports. I find their book very helpful when working with athletes at all levels, and recommend it to all who want to break through their barriers and reach new levels in life and sports."

—**Graham Betchart, MA**, mental skills coach and consultant to USA Basketball

"Whether it's to gain a mental advantage over the competition or to overcome performance anxiety, *Mindfulness for Student Athletes* can be integrated into every facet of an athlete's practice, game, and life."

—**Pete Kirchmer**, director of the University of California, San Diego's Center for Mindfulness mPEAK Program

"This workbook is a fantastic resource not only for student athletes, but also for individuals of all ages pursuing athletic endeavors. It is full of engaging activities as well as powerful messages to help instill confidence, learn how to manage stress, calm the mind, and improve performance. A must-read for student athletes!"

—**Stacie Cooper, MA, PsyD**, teen life coach, mindfulness and Pilates instructor, and author of *The Masks We Wear*

"Many professional athletes and Olympic medalists use mindfulness and visualization to enter into a state of flow, to de-stress, and to cultivate greater focus. Now, with this wonderful book, youth can utilize these same amazing techniques to excel at sports and to cultivate the many benefits of mindfulness for their personal lives in the process."

> —**Daniel Rechtschaffen, MFT**, director of Transformative Educational Leadership, and author of *The Mindful Education Workbook* and *The Way of Mindful Education*

"A wonderful book that gives any athlete of any sport a nimble, agile, and yet powerful set of skills to maximize performance and joy from the practice fields to the competitive places they boldly choose to go."

> —**Jeffrey Bernstein, PhD**, child and teen psychologist, and author of *Mindfulness for Teen Worry* and *10 Days to a Less Defiant Child*

"Biegel and Corbin's *Mindfulness for Student Athletes* is a brilliant workbook for students and coaches. How I wish my own daughter had this resource when she was a high school and collegiate runner. Mental well-being is a well-known key for athletic achievement, but achieving it is easier said than done. Gina and Todd help teens expertly explore the processes through which mental stability and athletic performance merge. Through thirty-two exercises, students learn for themselves how to address thoughts, emotions, senses, body awareness, fear, pressure, gratitude, and so much more. The authors share wisdom from dozens of renown athletes of a wide variety of sports. This accessible book is easy to understand, and students may find it hard to put down. I did!"

> —**Laurie Grossman**, director of program development and outreach at Inner Explorer, cofounder of Mindful Schools, and coauthor of *Master of Mindfulness*

"Biegel and Corbin have created a masterful workbook to help athletes bring mindfulness into their game and life. Through skill-building exercises and mindful behavior techniques, young athletes can learn to sharpen their focus, turn stress into motivation, and find ease in performance. *Mindfulness for Student Athletes* is an essential resource for young competitors and their coaches."

—**Whitney Stewart**, mindfulness instructor, and author of *Mindful Me* and *Mindful Kids*

"The life of a student athlete can be pressure-filled, with high stakes. Gina Biegel and Todd Corbin have created a resource that will be a great support for students hoping to find healthy ways to navigate the stress of competition, stay mentally balanced, and keep their head and heart in the game for all the right reasons."

—**Jennifer Cohen Harper**, mom, author, and founder of Little Flower Yoga and Mindfulness

"Sports are fun. At least they're supposed to be. But a student athlete can easily feel the acute pressure of performance and competition which turns fun into a high-stress situation. That, of course, gets in the way of both enjoyment and results. In *Mindfulness for Student Athletes*, Gina Biegel and Todd Corbin provide young athletes with a valuable structure and support plan to relieve stress, build confidence, and regain their original enjoyment of sport. A wonderful guidebook."

—**James Baraz**, coauthor of *Awakening Joy*, and cofounding teacher at Spirit Rock Meditation Center in Woodacre, CA

mindfulness for
student athletes

a workbook to help teens reduce stress & enhance performance

GINA M. BIEGEL, MA, LMFT
TODD H. CORBIN, CPC

Instant Help Books
An Imprint of New Harbinger Publications, Inc.

Publisher's Note

This publication is designed to provide accurate and authoritative information in regard to the subject matter covered. It is sold with the understanding that the publisher is not engaged in rendering psychological, financial, legal, or other professional services. If expert assistance or counseling is needed, the services of a competent professional should be sought.

Distributed in Canada by Raincoast Books

INSTANT HELP, the Clock Logo, and NEW HARBINGER are trademarks of New Harbinger Publications, Inc.

Copyright © 2018 by Gina Biegel and Todd Corbin
Instant Help Books
An imprint of New Harbinger Publications, Inc.
5674 Shattuck Avenue
Oakland, CA 94609
www.newharbinger.com

Cover design by Amy Shoup; Acquired by Jess O'Brien; Edited by Karen Schader

---

Library of Congress Cataloging-in-Publication Data

Names: Biegel, Gina M., author. | Corbin, Todd H., author.
Title: Mindfulness for student athletes : a workbook to help teens reduce stress and enhance
    performance / Gina M. Biegel, Todd H. Corbin.
Description: Oakland, CA : Instant Help, 2018.
Identifiers: LCCN 2018023095 (print) | LCCN 2018037576 (ebook) | ISBN 9781684030804 (PDF e-book) |
    ISBN 9781684030811 (ePub) | ISBN 9781684030798 (paperback)
Subjects: LCSH: Stress management for teenagers. | Mindfulness (Psychology) | Resilience
    (Personality trait) | Motivation (Psychology)
Classification: LCC BF724.3.S86 (ebook) | LCC BF724.3.S86 B539 2018 (print) | DDC 158.1/3024796--dc23
LC record available at https://lccn.loc.gov/2018023095

Printed in the United States of America

24   23   22

10   9   8   7   6   5   4   3

dedication

For all of the underdogs out there. Keep going, push through, find and open new doors.

—Gina Biegel

For Ben, Will, and all other student athletes everywhere, may you always bring your full presence and passion to every game, match, practice, or competition.

—Todd Corbin

contents

letter to student athletes

Odds are you probably love sports—the competition and the camaraderie that comes from playing. It can be exhausting and frustrating at times to be a student athlete. A lot of balls to keep in the air! Some key ways to improve as an athlete, as you probably know, are about dedicating time and energy to practice and training. Sports brings with it a lot of joy and excitement, but there can also be a lot of stress, pain, worry, and disappointment, to name a few.

Todd speaking here. Like you, I was a student athlete. I played mostly baseball and golf, but still found time for basketball, football, and tennis. I'm still a sports enthusiast and an avid runner. I spent many years coaching baseball. I'm what I'd call a "stress expert," coach and mindful motivator. I teach many of the skills in this book to student athletes because I know how beneficial it is to stay in the moment and not get carried away by your thoughts, emotions, or things you can't control.

This book is meant to supplement your athletic experience; it doesn't replace your practice sessions or training. Learning from coaches, teammates, and the like is critical for your athletic development and your potential success as an athlete. Through working on activities in this book, you'll be able to:

- reduce the impact that stress and anxiety have on your performance;

- boost your confidence and mental toughness;

- increase your ability to get into "the zone";

- calm your mind to gain an advantage on and off the athletic field;

- gain more control and awareness of your actions and emotions;

- enhance performance.

Each activity contains a core skill-building exercise, a brief *Game Time Mindful Takeaway*, and a *Something More* that offers additional ways to apply the core skill. There's plenty of room to jot down notes. You may even want to snap a photo of one of the many quotes from athletes or concepts you find motivational or helpful to better remember them or share them with a friend or teammate. There are also a host of materials available for download at the website for this book: http://www .newharbinger.com/40798. (See the back of this book for more details.)

Former NFL great Peyton Manning once said, "I never left the field saying I could have done more to get ready and that gives me piece of mind." We hope this workbook helps you prepare, reach, and even exceed your wildest sports dreams.

Warmly,

Todd Corbin and Gina Biegel

letter to coaches, parents, and professionals

Today, there is growing pressure for student athletes to succeed in all areas of their lives—not only at school, but also at home. It is challenging for adults to work with youth who are constantly being distracted and pulled in so many different directions. For coaches, parents, and the like, time to instill and teach needed athletic and life skills is often in short supply. The situation is made even more difficult in a world filled with social media, where social comparisons are ever present.

Student athletes face many unique challenges: managing their health and safety, their own expectations and those of others, parent-coach conflict, training time, financial burdens, and scheduling, to name a few. This workbook is designed as a resource to help your student athlete(s) better navigate the stresses, pressures, pain, and suffering that can arise from playing and practicing competitive sports. As you read this book, you'll be able to gain valuable insights to reduce the stress and worries that come from coaching, parenting, or working with youth.

Tailored for student athletes, the activities provide a research-based set of skills to:

- enhance performance;
- manage and reduce stress;
- increase sport satisfaction;
- boost confidence;
- decrease worry and anxiety.

This workbook is designed to offer a great deal of flexibility. It can be used with a single athlete or a group; during the off-season or with your team during the season.

There are thirty-two similarly structured activities that stand on their own. Select any activity that resonates and share it with your team or athlete during a practice session or team meeting, or after a scrimmage or preseason competition. Each activity contains a core skill-building exercise, a *Game Time Mindful Takeaway*, and a *Something More* that offers additional ways to apply the core skill. Additional materials can be downloaded at the website for this book: http://www.newharbinger.com/40798. (See the back of this book for more details.)

Activities 1–7 help student athletes recognize how stress impacts their performance, gain insight into their athleticism and decision making, and understand the benefits of being a mindful athlete.

Activities 8–32 focus on crucial skills for any student athlete to learn—skills that have the potential to provide athletes with a competitive edge. These activities focus on the physiological and psychological aspects of personal growth and development: those areas that help build mental toughness, sports confidence, emotional control, focus, positive attitudes of mind, good sportsmanship, and self-awareness.

We wish you the best on your quest of teaching the young men and women in your charge to be confident, resourceful, resilient, compassionate, and thoughtful student athletes.

Warmly,

Gina Biegel and Todd Corbin

the mindful athlete: what is mindfulness?   1

Kareem Abdul-Jabbar, the NBA's all-time leading scorer, said, "Your *mind* is what makes everything else work." It's the mind that allows everything else to fall into place to perform. Athletes prefer a mind that is confident, focused, and mentally tough, rather than one that is anxious, distracted, and out of control. However, at one time or another, all athletes feel like they didn't perform their best. Perhaps their minds or bodies felt off, or distractions made it hard to focus. This is where being a mindful athlete can help you.

Mindfulness is about being more aware of your thoughts, feelings, physical sensations, and the external environment in the present moment—and making better-informed choices about what you'll do, now, having this new awareness.

what is a mindful athlete?

According to *Merriam-Webster's Collegiate Dictionary* 11th edition, an athlete is "a person who is trained or skilled in exercises, sports, or games requiring physical strength, agility, or stamina."

Mindful athletes can find improved awareness of their minds and bodies, allowing for control and power over their choices. Look at the different areas that can improve when you bring mindfulness into your life:

awareness of physical sensations

Tuning into physical sensations can alert you to changes in your body and its potential for strength, agility, and stamina. For example, if you become aware that your shoulders feel stiff, you can do extra stretching to loosen up and hopefully perform better. Tennis players whose grip is becoming too loose might start missing shots wide right. Noticing this feeling in their fingers, they can make changes to tighten their hold on the racquet and start hitting more powerful, accurate shots.

What are some physical sensations you've noticed when you play a sport?

_____

_____

awareness of thoughts

Images or scenes, upsetting or pleasant memories, and past conversations that arise in one's mind are all going to impact how someone performs. Remembering a time when you finished a race in a very strong position and your coach told you how impressed she was with your determination can give you additional confidence to help you excel for the next competition. Similarly, thoughts such as _I'm doing awful today_ or _No way can I do this_ set you up to perform poorly.

What are some thoughts that often come up for you when you think about your ability or performance in sports?

_____

_____

_____

awareness of feelings

Your mind and body are connected, and one will often affect the other. Excitement over an upcoming game, frustration over playing time, worries about an opposing team or player, and confidence or doubt about how you'll do are all examples of feelings that will impact your performance. You might get angry when you feel that an opposing player's action is disrespectful to you or your team. Getting stuck in this anger can cause you to temporarily lose focus and make a mistake. Being mindful of feelings can help you release this negative tension so you can focus more clearly.

What are some feelings you often have around playing sports?

_____

_____

awareness of the external environment

Being aware of the conditions on the playing field, the social interactions from spectators or opposing players, and your input from senses—sights, sounds, or smells—are all environmental factors that can affect play. The more aware you are of noticing where your opponents are on the court or field, the better chance you'll have to react appropriately to protect the ball.

What are some things you can pay attention to in your external environment when you play or practice a sport?

_____

_____

why be a mindful athlete?

When you're already dedicating so much time to your sport(s) on practice and conditioning, in addition to actual games or performances, why bring mindfulness into it? You can train, practice, and sculpt your body so that it's full of strength, quickness, and endurance, yet still not be performing at your best. This could be because you're neglecting what's responsible for making everything else work—your mind!

How important do *you* think the mental side of your sport performance is: 10 percent, 20 percent, 50 percent, or more? Hall of Famer tennis great Chris Evert, who won 18 grand slam singles championships, said, "Ninety percent of my game is mental. It's my concentration that has gotten me this far."

Weight training and conditioning help build stronger physical muscles, but you also need to sculpt your mental muscles. Unlike having to go to the gym or weight room to work out your physical body, you can practice being mindful no matter where you are or what you're doing. This makes being mindful quite convenient. You'll begin to learn how to bring mindfulness into athletics and your life as you go through the activities in this workbook.

game time mindful takeaway   Bringing mindfulness into your life and athletics can improve your awareness of your physical sensations, thoughts, feelings, and the external environment. Improved awareness in these areas can help you tune into your performance. As you increase your mindful awareness, you might more easily notice a physical tendency in your opponent that you can exploit; realize and let go of some negative thoughts that have been causing you to struggle to keep your mental focus; or be able to make wiser split-second decisions on the playing field.

something more

Are you mindful or mindless? Circle any of the attributes that have applied to you at one point or another when you've engaged in sports.

When you are being *mindful*, you are more:

alert	mentally tough
balanced	present
confident	resourceful
creative	responsive
focused	thoughtful
insightful	

When you are not paying attention to this moment, being more *mindless*, you are more:

anxious	fearful
careless	irritable
distracted	out of control
doubting	reactive
easily injured	worried

Refer to these lists and consider the aspects of being a mindful athlete—your physical sensations, thoughts, feelings, and the external environment, when answering these questions.

Write down a specific time when you were playing a sport and felt more aware, in control, or *mindful.*

_____

_____

What do you remember about the overall experience?

_____

_____

Now write down a specific time where you felt out of control, or *mindless.*

_____

_____

What do you remember about the overall experience?

_____

_____

What differences in your performance, if any, did you notice when you were mindful and mindless?

_____

_____

_____

developing a sports portfolio 2

Nike, the large shoe and clothing company, is a master at getting people to buy its products through motivating ad campaigns or by finding the best professional athletes to partner with for promoting its brands. It's developed dozens of successful signature shoe lines in the past four decades in every sport imaginable.

How does Nike do it? They do their homework. Nike really understands the marketplace, recognizing which top athletes from which sports could help inspire the most innovative designs that people will want and buy. Nike does a lot of market research and analysis to know how best to spend its money and resources to improve its overall performance and that of the athletes who wear their products.

As a student athlete, when you do your homework and understand which of your sports and skills are your strongest and which could use improvement, you can learn and decide where to best put your attention and effort so you can maximize your potential. One day, you may even have your own signature shoe line!

developing your sports portfolio

Using the inventory below, circle all the sports you have ever played. Under "other," write in any you've played that aren't listed. Next, place a check by each sport you currently play or have played in the past year. Finally, put a star next to any of the sports you feel you have talent or skill in, or wish to perform at a higher level in the future.

Sports Inventory

archery	flag football	soccer
badminton	football	softball
baseball	golf	surfing
basketball	gymnastics	swimming
bowling	hockey	table tennis
cheerleading or competitive spirit squads	horseback riding	tennis
	lacrosse	track and field
cycling	martial arts	volleyball
cross-country	rowing	water polo
dance	rugby	weightlifting
diving	skating	wrestling
fencing	skiing	other: _____
field hockey	snowboarding	other: _____

List the sports(s) you're currently participating in that you wish to perform at a higher level, and possibly play collegiately or professionally. Refer to those you starred.

_____

_____

List some of your specific skills and talents that allow you to perform well for a given sport. Refer to those you starred.

_____

_____

_____

List some of the skills you'd like to improve in those sports you starred.

_____

_____

game time mindful takeaway   Developing a sports portfolio involves (1) reviewing the sports you play, (2) assessing the areas you're skilled or talented at, and (3) determining the areas that need improvement for growth. These steps can all help you in becoming a more mindful athlete. With this information, you can thoughtfully decide where you want to put your time and effort with the sport(s) you play.

something more:
the benefits of playing multiple sports

Professional baseball All-Star Giancarlo Stanton said, "I played basketball, baseball, and football. I never had much downtime. But I think playing multiple sports helped tremendously in my baseball career. I have the agility of all three combined into one."

While many students focus on playing only one sport, there are several benefits to participating in multiple sports. Playing a variety of sports can help you avoid burnout, reduce risk of overuse injuries, gain greater overall confidence, and develop better all-around skills. If you play one sport, consider the possibility of, and your interest level in, adding another sport.

Look back at the list of sports you put a check next to, and write down the ones you currently play.

_____

_____

Looking back at all the sports you circled above, are there any you've played in the past that you'd like to play again? If so, write them down here.

_____

_____

What new skills or enhanced skills could you gain from playing additional sport(s)?

_____

_____

_____

_____

Look back at your answers about which skills you still need to improve. How could the addition of a sport(s) help you with these skills?

_____

_____

_____

_____

3 your whys: what are your reasons for playing sports?

Muhammad Ali, one of the most celebrated sports figures of the twentieth century, said, "What keeps me going is goals." Whether in sports or life, have you ever felt like you didn't know which direction to go in? When you don't have a clear purpose, goals, or plans, you can be living your life aimlessly, almost on automatic pilot. Successful athletes understand the importance of having some clear goals and intentions for everything from practice and preparation to the actual games and seasons because that enables them to improve more quickly and most effectively.

get a better GRIP:
goals, reasons, intentions, and purpose

Each person has unique reasons, or whys, for playing sport(s). Knowing why you play the sport(s) you do and what you want out of your participation can help you figure out a clear purpose, goals, and plans.

Maybe you play a sport because you simply enjoy it or can spend time with your friends. Perhaps you play because your parents strongly encourage it or you're very good at the sport. Whatever your motivations, having solid reasons can help you stick with it when things get tough.

If you're playing multiple sports, select one for now and answer the following questions. List the sport you'll be focusing on here:

_____

G What **goals** would you like to accomplish in the sport this season?

Example: *Caroline wants to make the varsity team. She wishes she could be a starter. She also wants to finish in the top three.*

_____

_____

R What are your **reasons** for, or things that are most important to you about, playing the sport?

Example: *Mark finds it fun and likes the coach. He also gets to push himself physically.*

_____

_____

I **Intentions** are specific goals that have an extra amount of your personal energy behind them. What are your intentions in your sport?

Examples: *Paul intends to increase his shooting efficiency by 10 percent this season. Laura intends to trim five seconds off her best time. Claire intends to swing only at pitches she knows are in the strike zone.*

_____

_____

P Your **purpose** is your main reason, above all other reasons, for being a student athlete in the particular sport you play. Your purpose would have a great deal of meaning to you. What is your purpose for being a student athlete?

Example: *Leah wants to help her lacrosse team win a championship.*

_____

_____

a deeper dive into your goals

Three-time WNBA MVP Lisa Leslie knows the importance of setting and achieving goals: "Goal-setting and achieving those goals—that's just what I do."

How can you best use goal setting to your athletic advantage? There are three types of goals that emphasize distinctive aspects of your sport:

Outcome goals are bigger-picture goals not directly under your control.

Examples: *finishing first in a race; winning a tournament*

Performance goals are short-term objectives for specifics you want to achieve in your sport.

Examples: *wanting to beat a specific time; being able to make a particular number of passes*

Process goals identify the activities or processes you'll be engaged in while playing your sport.

Examples: *making a full turn with your shoulders each time you throw the ball; keeping your eyes focused on the ball every time it comes your way*

For one of your current sports, list at least one of each of these types of goals. Write down your sport here:

_____

An outcome goal for your sport is: _____

_____

_____

A performance goal for your sport is: _____

_____

_____

A process goal for your sport is: _____

_____

_____

game time mindful takeaway   Goals, reasons, and intentions usually change from season to season, or from year to year. However, your purpose, or main reason for playing, generally endures over a longer period. Identifying your GRIP helps provide a stronger foundation for being a mindful athlete.

something more:
goals outside of sports

You can use outcome, performance, and process goals for areas outside of sports. Choose a school subject or important activity in your life and reflect on different goals for it.

Write the subject or activity here: _____

An outcome goal for your subject or activity is: _____

_____

_____

A performance goal for your subject or activity is: _____

_____

_____

A process goal for your subject or activity is: _____

_____

_____

what stresses you? your opponent paper tigers 4

People, places, things, and situations in your life can invariably cause stress. What causes you stress depends on how you (1) *perceive* or view and (2) *appraise* or value the person, place, thing, or situation as stressful. In turn, your body responds physically or emotionally (or both) to the stressor. A *stressor* is something that is causing you stress.

fighting or fleeing tigers

Our ancestors needed to fight tigers in their paths—or flee from tigers to avoid being dinner. They also had to make critical decisions daily and decide how to approach possible rewards or avoid possible hazards. In preparing for hazards, our ancestors could make two mistakes: (1) thinking there was a tiger in the bushes when there wasn't or (2) thinking there was no tiger in the bushes when there was. The cost of the first mistake was needless anxiety. The cost of the second mistake was death. Our surviving ancestors were the ones that had a lot of anxiety—because they lived. You have evolved from a group of people whose brains were wired to make the first mistake a thousand times to avoid making the second mistake even once. Today, there are some drawbacks to this ancestral lineage:

- People can be overly alert, anxious, worried, and the like.

- The fight-or-flight response gets activated in many situations where it isn't needed.

- Over time, there is a cumulative buildup of stress hormones that, if not metabolized, can lead to many physical and psychological problems.

paper tiger paranoia

Psychologist Rick Hanson talks about *paper tiger paranoia*: that people today experience stressors as if they were encountering live tigers even though they are merely "paper" tigers that don't need to be fought or fled from. The same fight-or-flight response our ancestors experienced is initiated many times a day, even though you aren't meeting with real tigers. Your body responds to life stressors, these paper tigers, all the time, and you feel the effects mentally and physically as if you were encountering live tigers every day. Any stressful person, place, thing, or situation has the potential to stress you out in this way.

Do you know what your sports-related stressors are right now? Circle all that apply to you.

General Sports Stressors

competition among your peers for a spot on the team

not getting enough playing time

injury

pain

fear of "choking"

performance anxiety

playoffs/championships

time commitment

pressure to take it to the next level

a poor performance impacting the team

impacting peer, romantic, or family relationships

fundraising

Pressures You Feel from Your Coach

difference of opinion with your
    parents

what position you play

playing time

conflict about your participating in
    other activities

personality differences

win-at-all-cost coaching style

pressure to perform at a high level

Stressors Specific to Parents

pressure to perform well

need to get a scholarship

telling you how to play

not liking or getting along with your
    coach

being too vocal, embarrassing, or loud

difficulty getting rides

not being supportive

not being available or present

living through your athletic
    participation

game time mindful takeaway   Being aware of what your stressors
are and learning how they impact you physically and emotionally can help you
reduce your stress. Through the activities in this book, you can learn to approach
paper tigers as they are—merely paper and not alive. This can have a huge
impact on your performance and enjoyment for your sport.

something more:
the fight-or-flight stress response

On this diagram, mark where on your body you generally feel your stress.

Fight-or-Flight Stress Response

Normal or Relaxed State

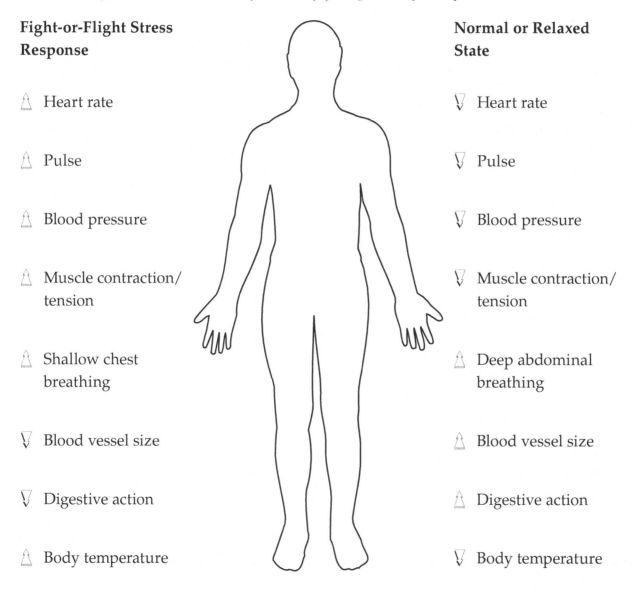

⌃ Heart rate

⌃ Pulse

⌃ Blood pressure

⌃ Muscle contraction/ tension

⌃ Shallow chest breathing

⌄ Blood vessel size

⌄ Digestive action

⌃ Body temperature

⌄ Heart rate

⌄ Pulse

⌄ Blood pressure

⌄ Muscle contraction/ tension

⌃ Deep abdominal breathing

⌃ Blood vessel size

⌃ Digestive action

⌄ Body temperature

Although the physical changes that take place when you're in fight-or-flight mode don't last long, stress does affect the body negatively over time.

the physical and emotional effects of stress on athletes 5

Stress presents red flags—cues that let you know when you are stressed. These cues may be physical or emotional. With awareness of your cues, you can recognize the onset of your stress and take steps to reduce it.

the physical effects of stress

Circle the symptoms you have when you're stressed. If you experience other physical problems that aren't listed, write them in.

change in body temperature

stomachache

nausea

faster heartbeat

heartburn

muscle tightness

sweating

trembling

tingling or numbness

headache

change in appetite

unusually rapid speech

change in weight

change in sleep habits

change in skin: dryness, itchiness, rash

chest pains

dizziness, faintness, or weakness

feeling of throat closing

shortness of breath or shallow breathing

heavy or faster breathing

racing or pounding heart

other: _____

other: _____

These effects are generally short-lived. Over time, stress can have more long-term negative effects on the body and impact most every physical health condition. It's important to keep your stress in check—minimizing how stressed you get can decrease the potential stress has in affecting your health and performance in the short and long run.

the emotional effects of stress

Think about the feelings you've experienced when you were stressed. Circle any of these feelings you have when you are stressed. If you experience other feelings that aren't listed, write them in.

angry	isolated or alone
anxious	overwhelmed
depressed	panicky
fearful	restless
frustrated	sad
hopeless	suspicious
hostile	worried
jumpy	worthless
nervous	other: _____
numb	other: _____
scared	other: _____

Reflect on which feelings are most common for you. For example, are you someone who gets angry or someone who tends to cry?

game time mindful takeaway   Pay attention to the red flags you physically experience and what emotions you generally feel when you're stressed, especially before or after a game or performance. Awareness of your mind and body can provide you necessary information to alert you to your stress so you can do something different to manage it.

something more

Now that you've had time to notice what physical symptoms and feelings you get when you're stressed, how do you express your stress more—physically or emotionally? Write down any feelings or thoughts that come up after going through this activity.

_____

_____

_____

_____

Look back over the physical symptoms and feelings you circled. In the table below, list those physical symptoms and feelings that you circled above.

Physical symptoms	Feelings
Example: Headache	*Example:* Worried

Now that you've completed this activity, you know what your red flags are.

When you notice one of these physical symptoms or feelings, remember it's a cue providing information that you're stressed. With this knowledge about your health—whether physical, emotional, or both—you can begin to make needed changes to feel better.

the athletic stress response 6

It's valuable to have an edge over your opponent in the sport you play; this edge can also help set you apart from other players. One quality that can contribute to your having an edge is being tuned into your stress level. You can then do something about it.

Stress impacts your performance in athletics. It can either help or harm you. The *athletic stress response* demonstrates a relationship between performance and stress. Some stress enables you to perform better—to a point. Once you hit this optimal point and stress continues to increase, performance sharply decreases.

when stress helps performance

Tanya, a softball player, finds that right before games her stomach often feels queasy. Her queasiness comes from the surge of adrenaline her body produces before games. Because she knows it's her body's way of getting ready for a game, she isn't scared or worried about it. She knows that the increase in her arousal and stress level is part of the athletic stress response. She finds that the adrenaline creates excitement, nerves, and curiosity about the unknown—and helps her perform better.

Tell about a time when stress helped you perform better or increased your motivation in athletics or elsewhere.

_____

_____

_____

_____

when stress harms performance

Jeremy, a hockey player, has noticed that right before games he gets a queasy stomach, although he doesn't know why. He gets so stressed about these stomachaches that he frequently can't sleep the night before a game. He's often exhausted and finds it hard to concentrate when playing. Sometimes he even vomits before the game because he has worked himself up so much about the game, and the unknown reason for his stomachaches.

This is an example of someone's stress being so high that it decreases performance. Because Jeremy doesn't know that the stomach queasiness is due to adrenaline—his body's natural response to getting ready for a game—his anxiety becomes so great that it begins to harm his sleep and his sports performance.

Tell about a time when stress harmed you and decreased your ability to perform or do well in athletics or elsewhere.

_____

_____

_____

_____

game time mindful takeaway
Learning your tipping point between when stress helps and when it harms you is a key to athletic performance.

something more

The 5 S's of Sports Training

Ken Doherty, a professional snooker player, says that "the 5 S's of sports training are: stamina, speed, strength, skill, and spirit." Write about how each of these has been or could be impacted by your stress.

Stamina _____

_____

Speed _____

_____

Strength _____

_____

Skill _____

_____

Spirit _____

_____

7 being in the zone

Have you ever been so immersed in an activity—playing sports, doing homework, surfing the Internet, playing a video game, or talking to a friend—that you focused solely on what you were doing and nothing else around you? You may have noticed that time seemed to slow way down. This is what performance psychologists call "being in the zone."

Being in the zone, as it relates to athletics, is being in a place where you're playing a sport at such a high level of skill and focus that everything automatically flows, and you're in tune with your mind and body. Greg Norman, who spent 331 weeks as the world's top-ranked professional golfer, described what being in the zone is like for him: "When everything is in sync, you feel like you are gliding through space. Things happen in slow motion. The wind feels different, the light is different, your eyesight is more acute. Each blade of grass seems to pop out. You've pushed yourself to the very maximum of your finely tuned ability to play."

how you can get into the zone

Athletes spend less than 10 percent of their time playing sports in this enhanced state. So what can you do as an athlete to get into the zone more often and stay there longer?

These conditions allow you to more readily experience being in the zone:

✓ when you are actively engaged in something you enjoy

✓ when you have a solid skill set in your activity that is balanced with the perceived challenge

✓ when your concentration is more completely on the activity rather than being distracted

✓ when there is clarity of goals

    ✓ when the experience itself is intrinsically rewarding

    ✓ when you have a feeling of control over the task

    ✓ when you aren't concerned with time

    ✓ when you're mindful

When you're mindful during sport practice or a game, you're playing in the moment—not thinking about the past, like a bad kick or shot, or the future, predicting how you are going to do—but about the current play. Being mindful helps you get or stay in the zone.

Let's look at times when you may have been in the zone. First, list some of the activities, sports and non-sports, you enjoy.

_____

_____

_____

Choose one of these activities and write about a specific time when you experienced being in the zone.

_____

_____

_____

What did you notice before, during, and after you were in the zone?

_____

_____

_____

Now that you've learned about some ways to be in the zone, list what you can do in your activity or sport to improve your chances of getting into the zone—and staying there.

_____

_____

_____

game time mindful takeaway   You increase your chances for being in the zone when playing your sport by being fully present to what is happening in the moment—being mindful.

something more

Boredom and Mind Wandering

Think of a recent class lecture, chore, or conversation where you were bored. Chances are, your focus on what was happening in that moment decreased, and your mind wandered.

Have you ever been bored during practice or a game? It's likely that when you were bored you didn't perform at a very high level. There are ways to move out of a bored, disinterested state. You need to shift or refocus your attention, notice something enjoyable or pleasant, or become aware of something new and novel. These actions can all bring you back into the moment and help you get into the zone.

Recall a specific time when you were bored during practice or a game. Then call, text, or message a friend or teammate to share the experience and what made it so boring. You might even discover others have felt the same way at times.

Now think of a few things you could have done to make the situation more interesting.

_____

_____

_____

_____

_____

8 sport sense awareness: tuning into your senses

Being in the zone—that is, in a state of focus where everything flows in tune with your mind and body—can positively impact your sports performance. In contrast, zoning out, daydreaming, and being on autopilot can negatively impact your performance in virtually anything you do—especially in sports. Paying attention to your five senses—what you see, smell, touch, taste, and hear—can bring you to the here and now. Being in the present can help you focus on what you're doing as you're doing it.

tune into your senses

The table that follows presents the responses of four student athletes who were part of a group asked to share their preferred sport and list all the different things they could be aware of for each of their senses.

Using their examples, circle all the senses that apply to your sport(s). Even if the sport listed isn't one you play, you may notice that sense when you play your sport(s).

Sense Awareness					
Sport	See	Smell	Touch	Taste	Hear
Volleyball	net, ceiling, lines, volleyball, asphalt, sky, outside, ref, air, jerseys, inside, knee pads, players, vents, people, spectators, sand, stands, ocean	sweat, knee pads, food from concessions, plastic, ocean, floor wax, sunscreen, air, ball	ball, water bottle, floor, net, stands sitting on, floor burns, clothes	sweat, popcorn, food, drink, blood, ball, net	cheering, screeching, noise on ground, talking, whistle, bouncing
Lacrosse	goal, grass, field, people, stick, big water jugs, crease in front of goal, uniforms, refs	grass, air, turf, plastic, ball's distinct smell, burning rubber, melted plastic on shoes	water on body and melting on your feet, other people, goggles, stick, gloves, grass, ground	sweat, victory, stick, mouth guard, sports drink	whistle, people, yelling, running, crying, feet on turf, grunting

| Baseball | bat, ball, gloves, diamond, other players, dugout, popcorn, bases, helmets, people on other teams, sand, cleats | popcorn, sweat, dust, glove, chalk from the lines, grass | glove, mitt, bat, ball, base, light, dirt, hands when high-fiving, water bottle | dirt, sweat, bubble gum, sunflower seeds, Gatorade | bat hitting the ball, sliding, yelling, cheering, strike three, sound of people running |
| Rowing | person in front of you, water, sky, sun, car, oar, trees, boat, logs floating in water, megaphones to hear coxswain | sweat, algae, dirt, cars, sunscreen | oar, side of boat, seat you are in sliding back and forth, if doing something wrong the water | water from water bottle, splash from person in front of you, sweat, sunscreen | yelling, sound of oar hitting the water, seat squeaking, boat not much noise, cars, wind, people |

Now, pick one of the sports you play. List it here: _____

With this sport in mind, list what you can see, smell, touch, taste, and hear when you're preparing and playing, and after you've finished. You can download a blank copy of this table at http://www.newharbinger.com/40798.

Sense Awareness					
Sport	See	Smell	Touch	Taste	Hear

Which of the senses is the strongest and most accessible to you?

_____

Which of the senses is hardest for you to notice?

_____

_____

Now that you know which of the five senses is strongest to you, when you want to be in the here and now, check in with your strongest sense first.

game time mindful takeaway   Paying attention to your senses allows you to be in the present moment. Being in the here and now can improve your focus, awareness, and clarity, greatly affecting your sports performance.

something more:
being mindful of activities

You can pay attention to your senses with any activity. When you're noticing any of the five senses, you're being mindful, because you're noticing that sense right now, in this moment. Mindfulness is all about being in this moment.

What activities are you involved in that you can bring sense awareness to by noticing your five senses? Here are some examples: hobbies, dance, music, a job. List a few activities here:

_____

Engage in an activity right now, and list everything you notice for each of the five senses. Write the activity here: _____

Sight _____

_____

Smell _____

_____

Touch _____

_____

Taste _____

_____

Hearing _____

_____

If you noticed anything that was different, new, or surprising to you, write about it here.

_____

_____

9 tuning into your visual anchor points

Michael Jordan, notably one of the greatest basketball players of all time said, "Focus like a laser, not a flashlight." Where you place your attention and focus during a game or practice will impact your sports performance. Learning to put your attention and focus on visual anchor points when you're stressed can help bring you into the present moment and center or redirect you away from your stress.

visual anchors

You can visually anchor your attention to something other than that which is causing you stress. Physical objects like these can be used as visual anchors when you are playing sports:

- nearby flag, sign, banner, or large tree branch

- lines on your playing surface

- nets, fences, or ropes

- light or speaker pole

- label, sticker, or tag on your clothes or equipment

- wristband you can touch or flick

- mouth guard you can bite down on or chew

- scoreboard

- bleachers, clubhouse, concession stand, seats, or benches

Paying attention to a visual anchor can:

- help you calm down;

- ease difficult feelings;

- reduce negative thoughts;

- bring you into the present;

- improve your attention and focus.

visual anchors practice

Following these five steps will help center and ground you before, during, or after a sporting activity. It might also help you begin to reduce and manage all stressful situations.

Step 1. Select any visual anchor point that you can readily see at any time—a seat, pole, shoes, or something else. You can use the list of visual anchors to guide you.

Step 2. Take a few seconds to observe the object. Notice its surface, shape, size, shine, texture, color, movement.

Step 3. While you're looking at the object, take a few slow deep breaths.

Step 4. If you become distracted, just bring your attention back to the object.

Step 5. Go back to what you were doing before this activity.

Complete the five steps on the previous page, and answer the following questions.

Before you paid attention to a visual anchor:

What was stressing you out? Consider what people, places, things, or situations might have been involved.

_____

_____

_____

What thoughts or feelings were you aware of that were stressful, difficult, or unsettling?

_____

_____

_____

After you paid attention to a visual anchor:

What object or objects did you use as your visual anchors?

_____

_____

_____

Has your stress changed? If so, how?

_____

_____

_____

What thoughts are present for you right now?

_____

_____

_____

What feelings are present for you right now?

_____

_____

_____

game time mindful takeaway   You can reduce your stress by paying attention to any visual anchors in your surroundings before, during, or after a sporting activity.

something more:
anchors you can touch

Adding touch to a visual anchor can boost its impact in grounding you to this moment. Ideally, you want an object that'll be easily visible and accessible to you during the whole sporting event.

For example, if you can touch an object like a shoe or wristband, touch it. If there's a brief pause in the game, consider adjusting your socks, or touching some item on your body—your shirt, pants, or wristband. During a timeout or break, look down at your shoes, untie them, and lace them back up; this visual anchor can help you slow an overactive or unsettled mind.

Some athletes even write a brief message on their shoes to help ground them and improve their focus.

Write down the anchor (or anchors) you plan to use. How will you use it?

Anchors:

_____

_____

_____

_____

How will you use them?

_____

_____

_____

_____

breathing through difficult moments 10

NBA champion Richard Jefferson notes the value of breathing through tough moments: "It has helped me mentally and physically. Just doing the breathing. Understand and feeling your body. It does a lot for you."

When stressed, athletes tend to hold their breath or otherwise restrict its natural flow. This creates a problem because, while you're trying to perform the moves required by your sport, your muscles are tensing up and other automatic physiological changes, like increases in sweat and blood pressure, are all taking place. This makes it difficult for your body to function and perform well if you are not breathing optimally.

what breathing through difficult moments means

We actually breathe about twenty thousand times each and every day. Breathing moves air though your entire body. You can use the information your breathing provides by tuning into your breath.

Breathing through is about:

(1) noticing your breath (is it flowing as it typically does or not?)

(2) taking a deep breath (this connects your mind and body)

(3) moving forward and coming to the next moment with a fresh perspective.

When you start breathing through a stressful moment, relying on your breath, you can change your stress level and the function of your mind and body.

when to breathe through difficult moments

You're breathing all the time, even when you aren't paying attention to it. Your breath can be a particularly useful grounding anchor to help you manage and move through difficult, unpleasant, and painful thoughts and feelings.

Here are some examples of situations you can breathe through: pain after a fall or injury; upset at losing a close game; embarrassment or upset for making a mistake; disappointment after a poor performance; anger at an official, player, or coach; and nervousness before, during, or after a performance.

how to breathe through difficult moments

Michael gets very nervous before most races. He starts thinking about what would happen if he cramped up during the race or didn't perform well. He tries to ignore his thoughts and worries, but they only make him feel worse. Michael's legs start to shake, and he notices that his breathing is short and shallow. The race hasn't even started yet. He then remembers the advice of his coach to breathe through difficult feelings.

Follow these steps:

Step 1. Smile.

Move your face muscles into a small smile and try to hold it for a moment.

Michael holds a small smile and finds that it makes him feel slightly better.

Step 2. Breathe deeply.

If you feel comfortable doing so, place your hands on your stomach, and notice your stomach move as you breathe. You can also place your hands by your side or on your lap. Just follow your breathing through your nose or mouth.

Michael places a hand on his stomach and takes a few deep breaths. He notices his stomach rising and falling.

Step 3. Follow the flow of your breathing.

Remember that, as you breathe, you are moving fresh air and oxygen to all the parts of your body.

Michael follows the flow of his breath, noticing it move though his body and legs. He finds it helps him calm down.

Step 4. Focus your breath.

You can focus your breath anywhere in your chest that you want to, especially in places where you might feel pain, stress, or tension.

Michael intentionally slows down his physical movements for a few seconds and continues to breathe through his legs, which had been shaking. He notices he's bringing clean air into his legs on his in-breath.

Step 5. Check in.

Notice how you are feeling now.

Michael finds that he's feeling much calmer and that his legs aren't shaking anymore.

Although you might not be experiencing a difficult moment while you complete this practice, try to remember to use it the next time you do experience a difficult moment.

game time mindful takeaway   *Breathing through* is a way for you to tune in and assess your current functioning, and move through it where appropriate. It does *not* mean ignoring or disregarding physical pain, like playing through an injury. When your breathing isn't flowing normally, this can be a cue to make a change or adjustment to the people, places, things, or situations that are causing you stress, pain, and suffering.

something more

After completing the five-step practice, answer these questions:

What did it feel like to smile while you were engaging in a physical activity?

_____

_____

What did you notice when you breathed deeply?

_____

_____

What area or part of the body did you focus your breath on? _____

What thoughts came up for you?

_____

_____

_____

What feelings came up for you?

_____

_____

_____

Describe how breathing through made your body and mind feel.

_____

_____

_____

What does breathing through mean to you?

_____

_____

_____

11 the 3-second rule practice: a mindful centering approach

Former MLB manager Terry Collins said, "The idea is to slow down. Slow the heart rate down; slow the thinking process; slow it down. Instead of rushing, take a second, take a breath, and assess what's going on here."

Your mind and body provide you with useful information. When you're aware of this information, you can make needed changes to help center yourself, calm down, get you in the zone, and get out of your head if you are stuck there.

the 3-second rule practice

This practice asks you to spend three seconds checking in on each of three focal areas:

- your mind

- your body

- your heart rate (HR) + breath (B) = HRB

Engaging in this practice allows you a quick, accessible way to check in with yourself, providing you with useful information such as:

- Checking in with yourself so you know how you're doing at any given moment. With this information, you can make adjustments, as needed, to change how you're doing physically or emotionally.

- A way to help you focus and center yourself in practice and during games.

- Having a mindful centering approach that helps you slow down and connect to your mind and body. This can positively impact your timing, ability, and performance in sports.

It takes only nine seconds in total to check in with your mind, body, and HRB, which will give you a good read on your current status. If you're doing well, keep doing it. If you're doing poorly, consider what adjustments you can make.

3-second rule practice

Step 1. Right now, spend three seconds noticing your *mind.*

Notice what thoughts are present for you, if any.

Notice what feelings or emotions are present for you, if any.

Step 2. Right now, spend three seconds noticing your *body.*

Scan through your entire body noticing what feels normal, different, hurt, sore, loose.

Notice any other sensations that are present in your body.

Step 3. Right now, spend three seconds noticing your *heart rate and breathing: HRB.*

Your heart rate and breathing are inherently connected. As you breathe in, your heart rate speeds up; as you breathe out, your heart rate slows.

Notice this connection between your heart rate and breathing.

game time mindful takeaway   The next time you are engaging in a sport, use the 3-Second Rule to check in with your mind and body so that you can make helpful changes.

debriefing the 3-second rule practice

Answer these questions to debrief this practice:

What was on your mind? What thoughts or feelings were present?

_____

_____

_____

What did you notice as you scanned your body?

_____

_____

_____

What did you notice about your heart rate and breathing?

_____

_____

_____

something more

You aren't limited to using the 3-Second Rule only for sports. You can practice the 3-Second Rule any time you want.

Think of some times where it might be useful to practice the 3-Second Rule; for example, before a test or homework, or when you're in an argument. Write down any people, places, things, or situations in your life when this practice could be useful.

_____

_____

_____

Think about one of these you just wrote, and write it here. _____

Now do the 3-second rule practice with this in mind.

Spend three seconds on your mind, body, and HRB. Ask yourself the following questions to assist you in this practice.

mind

What are you thinking about?

_____

_____

_____

Are your thoughts about the past, now, or future? _____

Are your thoughts judgmental? _____

What are you feeling right now? _____

_____

Do you have a hard time knowing how you are feeling right now?

_____

Is your feeling one you don't like or don't want to have?

_____

Write down a pleasant emotion you are feeling (for example, happiness, joy, contentment, peace).

_____

Write down an unpleasant or difficult emotion you are feeling (for example, sadness or anger).

_____

body

What do you feel in your body?

_____

_____

_____

Does anything ache or hurt? If so, what is it?

_____

Do you notice a pain you didn't know was there before? _____

Where are you located right now?

_____

What position is your body in (standing, sitting, lying down)?

_____

What time of day is it? _____

Are you inside or outdoors? _____

heart rate + breathing (HRB)

Is your heartbeat fast, normal, or slow? _____

Does your breath feel restricted, normal, sharp, shallow?

_____

Did you notice your heart beating when you noticed your breath? _____

Did you observe your stomach moving up and down as you were breathing?

_____

Did you notice your chest moving? _____

Was it hard to notice your breath without changing it? _____

Were you able to get to a point when you noticed your breath without changing it?

_____

12 CPR for choke prevention

It isn't always clear why some athletes perform better under pressure than others. The increased stress of having to make a penalty kick, sink a putt, get a hit, or strike a winning serve when the game is on the line can cause an athlete to choke. Choking in sports can also happen when an athlete or team is highly favored to win but doesn't, or is leading near the very end of the game and instead loses. You can greatly reduce the stress of such pressure situations by using a mindful strategy called CPR. Jay's story is an illustration:

Jay is feeling really nervous. He starts to bite his fingernails while on the bench during a timeout. In a moment he'll need to sink two free throws to tie the game in regulation. His arms and legs start to feel heavy, and his stomach lurches.

Jay checks in with himself, sensing the tightness he feels in his body while also noticing where his mind is focused. He watches his thoughts for a moment and becomes aware of how focused he is on what will happen if he misses the shots. He pauses for a moment, looks at his shoelaces, and takes a few deep breaths. This starts to relax him. He looks back at the basket and bounces the ball three times. This allows him to reset. He then refocuses his mind on his objective—getting the ball through the hoop.

how to perform well under pressure using CPR

CPR is an acronym that stands for an important life-saving technique. When an athlete is facing a high-pressure situation, CPR can also be quite useful. In this case, however, we aren't referring to a life-or-death matter—though many athletes might think that it is. In the context of athletics, CPR stands for **c**hecking in, **p**ausing with a breath, and **r**esetting, then **r**efocusing.

C Checking In

Take a moment and become aware of what you notice in your body and your mind: your thoughts and feelings. Checking in with yourself brings you to the here and now; you're paying attention to how you feel in the present rather than what happened or what might happen. Being in this moment can prevent additional stress.

P Pausing with a Breath

Pause by taking a breath (or a few breaths), and notice your breath as it is flowing. Pausing helps you relax and in turn will calm your mind down from any racing thoughts.

R Resetting and Refocusing

Resetting means starting your pre-shot or preparation routine again. It's the batter getting back in the batter's box after a big swing and a miss, or the tennis player bouncing the ball again and adjusting her feet, preparing for a second serve after a fault. When you're getting stuck in your mind or having a hard time concentrating, resetting brings you back to the present moment.

To refocus, you direct your mind back to your desired outcome. You might ask yourself, *What do I want to happen now?* It's always best to focus and refocus on what you want, instead of what you don't want. For example, a batter would focus on making a good swing instead of on not making an out.

CPR allows you to trust in your body to perform in a more calm, relaxed manner.

let's practice CPR

Imagine you are engaging in your sport of choice.

My sport is _____

Note: If the equipment you normally use (for example, club, bat, glove, stick, ball) is handy and you have enough space to use it, grab it. If not, just imagine this equipment.

The motion I normally make with my body while playing this sport is

_____

_____

As you use your equipment (or engage in a motion specific to your sport or activity), tighten and tense your muscles. For example, if you're a swimmer, try tightening your leg or arm muscles and mimic your swimming strokes. Focus on the feeling of the movement and watch what happens in your body as you make those restricted motions. Also notice what happens with your breathing as you tighten your muscles and how your mind responds with your thoughts and feelings.

   Check in now and feel what is happening in your body: arms, legs, and muscles. Also, check in with your mind and notice now what thoughts or feelings are present.

   Pause to notice your immediate surroundings, and take a few deep, relaxing breaths.

   Reset and **R**efocus by bringing yourself back to this moment. Feel the physical sensations as you make this same motion as before, but now with relaxed rather than tight muscles. Notice what the same action feels like when your muscles are relaxed and how much more focused you're able to be with your mind.

What did you notice during this exercise?

_____

_____

_____

Did you feel any difference between engaging in your sports movements with tight muscles versus relaxed muscles? If so, what were the differences?

_____

_____

_____

How might CPR help you during an important moment in a game?

_____

_____

_____

game time mindful takeaway   Remember to check in, pause with a breath, and reset, then refocus. The CPR practice helps keep your stress and tension down to a manageable amount so you will be less prone to choking under pressure.

something more

The next time you are watching sports, whether live or on TV, pay particular attention to how the athletes respond when the game or match is on the line, or in other pressure situations. Notice anything they do that helps them reset and refocus. You obviously cannot see if they're checking in with their minds, but you can probably tell if they pause and take an extra breath. For those athletes who seem to be choking under pressure, notice what is happening to the physical motions of their bodies.

Now think about some specific instances, perhaps where you would experience the most pressured situations, where you could use this CPR practice in your sport, and list them below.

_____

_____

_____

_____

_____

2BSET model of awareness

US Olympic track and field bronze medal winner Kellie Wells said, "If you think you can't, you won't, and if you think you can, you will. When I'm tired at practice, I tell myself that I'm not tired, and I can push through. If you tell yourself you're tired or if you tell yourself you're sick, your body is going to follow the mind."

Athletes need to be aware of many things to perform at their best, whether it's deciding where best to position themselves to defend a shot, selecting which person to throw the ball to, or like Kellie Wells, deciding how to talk to themselves so they can stay alert.

To be more mindfully aware, there are five main things to consider—(1) your breath, (2) your body, (3) your senses, (4) your emotions, and (5) your thoughts.

using the 2BSET model of awareness: breath, body, senses, emotions, and thoughts

1. **Breath:** Your breath has the capacity to increase your awareness by calming you down when you're agitated or energizing you to make you feel more alert.

   Before you next take the field or court, take a minute and just notice your breath without trying to change it. When your mind wanders, bring it back to the sensations of your breath.

2. **Body:** Your body communicates through sensations—a pain in your leg, an empty feeling in your stomach, a sudden rush of anger, or tightness in your face. For athletes, it's incredibly helpful to notice these internal signals.

   Take a moment to feel your feet on the ground, notice where your hands and arms are, the connection of clothing to your skin, and the sensations in and around your eyes.

3. **Senses:** Your senses—sights, sounds, smells, tactile feelings, even tastes—allow you to get vital information from your surroundings. Being aware of your senses can help you key in on things you may have missed in your physical environment.

   For the next minute, experience your senses. Notice one thing you see, hear, smell, feel, and taste. Even just noticing silence or the absence of a sense (for example, no taste) is helpful. Listen to the sounds you make as you play, feel the liquid from your bottle quench your dry mouth, or smell the aromas or unpleasant smells from practice around you.

4. **Emotions:** Emotions have the power to energize you, while also having the power to make you feel down. Often when you're under pressure to perform, your emotions can grab hold. By noticing your feeling as you're feeling it and labeling it (anger, frustration, nervous excitement), you can help calm stressful emotions down.

   Check in and notice what you're feeling emotionally right now. Maybe you recently finished up a practice, were watching a game or getting ready to play a game, or are just chilling. Are you happy, excited, sad, nervous, discouraged, or calm? Notice how the intensity of the feeling changes over time without you trying to do anything other than experience it.

5. **Thoughts:** People have sixty to seventy thousand thoughts a day—about forty-five thoughts every minute. If you are staring at the goal during a penalty shootout, it can seem like all forty-five of those thoughts are coming at once. Just noticing your thoughts can help slow them down so that you can then better trust your body to perform as it should.

   Watch your thoughts like clouds floating by in the sky, and notice what you are thinking about right now.

game time mindful takeaway   Tuning into your body, breath, senses, emotions, and thoughts can help ground you in the present moment so you can become much more mindfully aware of all the things in and around you. This can help reduce stress and enhance your overall performance.

something more

Think of a recent sports situation where you felt angry, sad, excited, or happy. Now, notice where in your body you most strongly experience that feeling. If you chose a time when you were angry, perhaps you felt the anger most in your chest or hands. If you selected a time when you were happy, maybe you felt it most in your face or heart area.

Next, take a few breaths. As you do, imagine moving your breath into the area of your body where that feeling is strongest. The breath can help "soften" that emotion.

The next time you are at practice or before a game, try the 2BSET model of awareness, bringing your awareness to your breath, body, senses, emotions, or thoughts.

14 mindfully drinking sports drinks and water

You might not realize that drinking water is more important than eating food, especially when your stomach scolds you for not having eaten anything since way before your last practice or game. We can actually live for almost a month without food, but we cannot go more than three days without drinking fluids.

why hydration is so important to your success as an athlete

Proper hydration can help you maximize performance, improve your ability to recover quickly from training or a competition, and minimize injury and muscle cramps. Even the American College of Sports Medicine understands how important water is to your performance: they recommend drinking four to eight ounces of water every fifteen to twenty minutes of exercise as a good starting point for hydrating athletes.

mindfully drink your sports drinks or water

If you already have or can get some water, a sports drink, or another beverage, do the following. Otherwise, follow these six steps the next time you take a drink of water or your favorite sports drink or beverage.

Step 1. Before you take a drink, take a breath and notice how your body and mind feel. Notice your level of thirst, and how hot, sweaty, or tired you are.

Step 2. Just prior to taking a mouthful of liquid, notice how the container feels in your hand. Is it cool or warm against your skin? Wet? Sticky?

Step 3. Notice what you see—the colors of the drink and the bottle, what's on the bottle or label, and any smells from the liquid. What shape is the bottle? What does the label look like?

Step 4. Feel the sensation of your lips and mouth as you drink, and notice how the liquid feels as it moves down your throat. Hear the sound as you drink.

Step 5. Notice how your body and mind feel now that you've had some liquid to hydrate your self.

Step 6. Take another drink and notice what changes, if any, you notice now in your body or mind.

game time mindful takeaway   Mindfully drinking a sports drink or water can bring you back into the present moment, especially after you have a particularly tough challenge during your game, competition, or practice. The next time you take a hydration break during a game or practice, remember to use your five senses to explore what it feels like to actually take a sip of sports drink or squirt of water.

something more

Mindful drinking is a skill you can use at any time during your day, not just during or after a sports activity. The next time you sit down for a meal or snack and have some kind of liquid refreshment, use the six steps presented in this activity to mindfully explore the beverage you have in front of you. Pay particular attention to how you feel before you take a drink, during the actual drink, and after you've had some of the beverage.

mindfully walking the lines in sports 15

Professional dancer and choreographer Martha Graham said, "All that is important is this one moment in movement. Make the moment important, vital, and worth living. Do not let it slip away unnoticed and unused."

Whether you are on the ice, field, mat, or track, or in the water, noticing your body and the movements you make is key to your overall sports performance. A great way to notice your body, improve focus, and calm your mind is to walk mindfully.

This activity is about mindfully walking in your sporting environment, focusing on the actual lines that are present. It can also apply to whatever movement is part of your sport; for example, swimming or skating.

mindfully walking the lines during sports practice

Read these instructions through before you begin your practice. The next time you are practicing, playing, or near the lines of your sport, do the following:

- Notice the lines or boundaries on your playing surface. It could even just be the edge of the mats on the gym floor, or the border between the golf fairway and rough.

- For three to five minutes, before or after a practice or a game, or another time when you are on your own, mindfully walk the lines, silently, and at your own pace. For example, mindfully walk, swim, or skate, along the lines of your playing surface. Start anywhere that is comfortable to you. It isn't necessary to change your breath in any way; just breathe naturally.

- Remind yourself that this practice isn't about speed or trying to get anywhere; consider moving slowly.

- Notice your physical sensations as you move your feet, legs, hands, and arms, and your body as a whole.

- Notice the feeling of your feet as you move on or alongside the lines of your sport.

- Just as you might occasionally step off the lines, your mind might wander to random thoughts, a noise, or mind chatter.

- When you notice you are distracted:

    Notice what it is that is distracting you.

    Pause the movement.

    Give the distraction attention. You might try stopping for a moment, noticing your surroundings.

    Resume the practice when you are ready.

    If you're still having a hard time redirecting your attention, focus on the sensations of your feet on the ground.

debriefing: mindfully walking the lines in sports practice

What sport did you mindfully walk the lines of? _____

Does your sport have traditional lines, or did you have to figure out the "lines" you could follow? Explain here.

_____

_____

What was this experience like? _____

_____

_____

What thoughts came up for you as you moved? _____

_____

_____

What feelings came up? _____

_____

_____

If your mind wandered, were you able to bring your focus back to the practice?

_____

Do you remember what you focused on to redirect your attention to the practice? If so, explain here. Note: What helped refocus you can possibly be used to refocus your attention in future practices.

_____

_____

game time mindful takeaway   The next time you take the field or court, pay attention to the lines and boundaries of the sport you play and mindfully walk the lines. This practice can bring you into the present moment, help get you into a good rhythm, feel calmer, and into the present moment, where the zone awaits.

something more:
mindful walking practice

You can practice mindful walking in any setting by paying attention to your body sensations as you walk. It's about noticing your body and using it to anchor, ground, and center you in the present moment. When you pay attention to any aspect of the walking, you're paying attention to the present. The interesting part about mindful walking is that it isn't about getting anywhere or attaining any goal, which is often counter to movement in sports; it's just about the walking.

One of the most important sensations to notice is the feeling of your feet touching the earth and grounding you to this moment. It's also about paying attention to the turning at the end of the path. It's a grounding practice that brings you into the present moment through movement in your body.

When you notice your thoughts and feelings while walking, you can redirect your attention back to the walking and specifically bring attention to your feet. Your feet are the farthest thing from your head. When you get distracted in thoughts or feelings that aren't productive, you can always turn to the sensations of your feet touching the earth. When you're engaged in the mindful walking practice, you aren't necessarily thinking about what happened or what is going to happen, but your attention is on what is occurring right now, as it is taking place: the walking.

To do this practice, follow these directions:

- Pick a path about ten to fifteen feet long.

- Walk the path back and forth, not at any particular speed.

- Remind yourself that you aren't trying to get anywhere, just noticing your physical sensations as you walk.

- When you notice you are distracted you can:

    Notice what it is that is distracting you.

    Pause the walking.

    Give the distraction attention.

    Resume the walking practice when you are ready.

    If you're still having a hard time redirecting your attention, focus on the sensations of your feet on the ground.

Think of the different places and times you can try mindful walking and list them here:

_____

_____

_____

_____

You can do this mindful walking practice anytime you want in a safe environment.

16 mindful stretching and warm-ups

Four-time Super Bowl MVP and champion Tom Brady said this about mindful stretching: "It's great for flexibility, it's therapeutic, and great for your attitude."

Many people, athletes and nonathletes alike, wear headphones and listen to music, watch TV, read, or chat with friends while lifting weights, warming up, working out, or stretching. Some use these things as a distraction from the actual activity (ever blast music while you're doing homework?) while others use them as motivation to work out harder. While there is nothing inherently right or wrong in doing any of these things, it can sometimes make it more difficult for you to be aware of your body during the activity.

Why is this awareness important? Paying attention to the physical sensations of your body is one of the key mindfulness skills we've been discussing that helps you stay in the moment. When you aren't as aware of your body as you could be, you may be more prone to stress, emotional upset, pain, or injury.

Ken Katich, who is known throughout the NBA as the "yoga guy," believes it's vital for athletes to become very aware of their bodies. He has said that many professional athletes simply don't know their bodies' strengths and limitations well enough, which may lead to doing things that can cause pain and injuries. As we've discussed in earlier activities, your body communicates with you through its physical sensations. The more you tune into the sensations, the better you'll know your body. This knowledge will allow you to make adjustments almost automatically and help improve sports performance.

about mindful stretching and warm-ups

Mindful stretching or warming up is about engaging in exercises and body movements while paying attention to the physical sensations of the muscles you're using. It's about holding the stretches long enough to allow the muscles to lengthen. This increases muscle flexibility and joint range of motion. Warming up mindfully allows you to calm and balance yourself, which can be incredibly helpful, especially if you feel nervous or anxious playing in a big game or tournament.

You can do mindful stretching while standing, sitting, or lying down. You can do it during a practice or before a game, after sitting too long at your desk, or anytime your body feels a little tight. Whether you're stretching your legs out before a race or your arms before getting ready to throw, mindful stretches help you tune into your body and prepare for physical activity.

standing mindful stretching practice

Stand upright with your feet firmly rooted to the floor, your knees slightly bent, and your arms resting at your sides. Your body weight should be evenly distributed on the bottoms of both feet. While looking straight ahead, bring your arms up slowly from the sides and reach upward to the ceiling (or sky) with your palms facing inward toward each other. As you bring your arms up, breathe in deeply. Pause for a few breaths, and feel the stretch in your arms, hands, fingers, legs, feet, toes, shoulders, back, and neck. Hold this pose for a few seconds, then bring your arms back down while you exhale fully. Repeat this exercise a few times, each time pausing at the top for a few breaths.

What did you notice while doing this exercise?

_____

_____

Now, do this same standing exercise, but this time do it quickly without really paying any attention to your body, movement, or muscles. You might even want to distract yourself by watching TV or chatting with a friend.

What did you notice as you did this rapidly without much awareness of your body?

_____

_____

How did your attitude change, if at all, while doing the stretching first with mindful awareness and then without?

_____

_____

lying down mindful stretching practice

Lie on your back with your arms at your sides, and take a few deep, relaxing breaths. Pay attention to all the connection points of your body to the floor or ground. Gently pull your right knee toward your chest while straightening your left leg to the floor. Hold for seven breaths. Now do the same thing with your left knee, straightening your right leg to the floor. Remember to keep breathing fully, paying particular attention to the feeling of the muscles as they stretch.

game time mindful takeaway   The main things to mindful stretching are to pay attention to the range of motion and feeling in the muscles as you're doing the movement and to hold the stretches for at least a few breaths. It will be helpful to notice what's happening in your body if you do the stretching or warm-ups in silence for at least a minute.

something more:
a mindful warm-up practice

US Olympic gold medalist Florence Griffith-Joyner understands the importance of warming up before a competition or game: "A muscle is like a car. If you want it to run well early in the morning, you have to warm it up."

List one or two warm-up activities that you do for a particular sport you play.

(1) _____

(2) _____

To mindfully warm up in your chosen sport, bring your attention to the feeling in your body as you engage in the activity, whether it is passing, shooting, catching, throwing, swimming, running, or kicking.

While doing your warm-up activity, pay attention to the motion of your body, the feeling of the equipment on your skin, and how your legs and arms move. Occasionally check in with what's happening in your mind as you're warming up. Maybe it's relatively calm and quiet; maybe it's filled with lots of thoughts about the upcoming game or a previous practice session. If you notice yourself getting caught up or distracted by your thoughts while warming up, bring your focus back to the physical sensations of and in your body. This will help you get the most out of your warm-up session.

17 taking a short break: sitting body scan practice

Joe Johnson, seven-time NBA All-Star, finds yoga is his time to commune with both his body and his mind: "[Yoga is] meditation and therapy for my muscles…because the better you treat your body, the more longevity you'll have."

It's important to frequently take a break and check in with your body and mind. It can be easy to often overlook one or both. When you're tired, stressed, worried, overwhelmed, and the like, it's easy to zone out. When you catch yourself being zoned out, this is a good time to do a sitting body scan practice and zone back in.

sitting body scan mindfulness practice

The sitting body scan mindfulness practice helps you check in with yourself, recharge, and feel less stressed. You can do this practice anytime you want, as long as it doesn't interfere with the activity you're involved in. This practice can be beneficial when you are

- sitting on the bench or ground before or during a game or practice;

- in the locker room before or after a game or practice or during a half-time or break;

- in class before a test;

- going to do your homework;

- trying to make a difficult decision (it can help you respond instead of react);

- in a disagreement with someone.

To get the most out of the experience, the recommendation is that you spend five minutes, but you can do it faster if necessary. You can keep your eyes open or closed. At first, you'll probably have to read these directions before you start or during the practice. Over time, it is intended that you can scan through your body without these written instructions. You can record these directions on your phone or some other device. Then, you can listen to them whenever you want.

practice instructions

before you begin

- Get into a comfortable seated position. Notice where you are sitting. Pay attention to what your body is in contact with.

- Observe what is around on you. Pay attention to your five senses. What can you see, smell, hear, touch, and taste?

- Be like a detective in your own body; just notice what is going on in your body right now. As you move throughout your entire body, you might notice a pain or sensation you hadn't before, especially if you had a tougher practice or game earlier in the day. You might recognize a familiar feeling. You might notice nothing at all. Any and all experiences and feelings that are present are normal and natural.

begin your practice: lower body

- Bring your attention to both of your feet: your toes, the tops and bottoms of your feet, the balls of your feet, and your heels. If you are wearing shoes, feel the connection of your feet to them.

- Proceed to your ankles, noticing the connection between your feet and your lower legs. Attend to your calf muscles and shinbones. Then move up to your knees as they connect to your upper thighs. Notice both hamstring and quadriceps muscles.

- Move up to your hips, and notice both feet and legs in their entirety. Be aware of what you recognize along the way. You don't have to flex your muscles or change what is. Just monitor what is present.

- Pay attention to the support that both feet and legs provide you.

continue your practice: upper body

- Now move up to your stomach and chest. Notice your stomach and lungs expand and release as you breathe.

  Reminder: You do not need to change your breath in any way; simply notice your body just as it is. You may find that your breath does change; this is normal. Over time, your breathing will shift as you gain experience doing this practice.

- Move your attention from your chest up to your collarbone and shoulders.

- Now, bring your attention all the way down to the tips of your fingers. Witness the air that surrounds your fingers and what the air feels like on the tops and palms of your hands.

- Move from your hands to your wrists and up to your forearms, elbows, and upper arms, noticing both bicep and tricep muscles. Recognize what is present along the way and the support that your hands and arms provide you.

- As you reach your shoulders, bring your attention down to your lower back, and notice what your lower back is in contact with. Notice your spine and the spaces between your vertebrae as you move up your back to your neck and shoulders.

- Let go of any tension you might be holding in your shoulders. Release any muscles that are engaged here. Let your shoulders, arms, and hands go loose if you can.

- Move up from the back of your head to the front of your face. Release any facial expression you might have. If your jaw is clenched, release it.

- Notice all the parts of your face. Now bring your attention from your face down to your throat and then to your heart. Try to feel your heart beating.

- Now, take in all you notice in your entire body. Breathe in fresh air and calmness on the next in-breath, and release any tension in any area of the body you would like on the next out-breath.

practice close

- Begin to wiggle your fingers or toes.

- If your eyes are closed, gently open them and allow the light to enter.

You have now completed the sitting body scan mindfulness practice. You can choose to take a piece of how you feel right now with you to the rest of your day.

Game Time Mindful Takeaway   Each time you do the sitting body scan mindfulness practice, your experience will be different. There is no right or wrong way to feel during or after this practice. You might label a practice as good or bad, but remember that whatever you experience is normal. Try this practice in a number of different situations, and continue to use it when you find it helpful.

something more:
lying down body scan mindfulness practice for sleep

Do you ever have a hard time falling asleep because thoughts about a tough game or practice or your to-do list are circling around in your head? Are there other times when you have a hard time settling down to sleep? If you answered yes to either question, then the lying down body scan mindfulness practice for sleep is just for you.

Here are the steps:

- Turn off any electronics, such as phone, TV, and computer.

- Get into a comfortable position lying on your bed. It can be helpful to get into the position you like to sleep in.

- Now, bring awareness and focus on the different areas of your body that you can notice, from the tips of your toes to the top of your head. Check in with these areas:

  toes and feet

  legs and hips

  stomach and chest

  hands, arm, and shoulders

  back and neck

  head and face

- After you have scanned your entire body, notice how you feel.

You can repeat this process anytime you like. If your thoughts are still looming in your head, take a notepad and write them down. Now that they're on paper, try to let them go.

mindful preparation and managing routines 18

NBA superstar LeBron James understands the power of mindful preparation and managing routines: "When you're prepared and you're well prepared, then you have a lot of confidence going into a game. It's all about the process."

You need to put in the work (your mental and physical preparation and routines) in order to be ready to perform; when you do, your level of confidence will increase. The result is enhanced performance and a feeling of being in control.

The primary goal of mental preparation is to allow you to play with confidence. The primary goal of physical preparation and having a consistent routine is so your body can be ready to play more skillfully and reliably. Adding mindfulness to your preparation and routines helps keep you focused on the present moment, which is when you can play your best. The most successful athletes, like LeBron James, are students of the game; they study and plan and prepare mentally and physically with a great deal of mindful awareness.

getting mindful about your preparation and routines

How you approach your practice sessions and preparation for games is one of the keys to being a successful athlete. Some of that certainly has to do with your coach and your training regimen, but a lot has to do with your attitude.

The next page contains a list of things that help athletes prepare for a game, match, or competition. Circle any you currently do. Next, place a check by any you don't currently do but would like to add to your own mental or physical preparation. If there are some things you do that aren't listed, write them next to the "other" category.

hydrate

ice body/muscles

take a nap or get extra sleep

warm up (for example, batting practice, shooting drills, laps)

watch game films

review scouting reports

go for a run

have or bring a snack or eat a special meal

review playbook or player notes

have correct equipment

test equipment

bring backup equipment

dress appropriately for weather

have good shoes/cleats

get body or legs taped or wrapped

visualize winning moments

listen to music

join teammates for dinners

other: _____

other: _____

A routine is a predetermined series of actions that help get your mind and body ready to perform and take the randomness out of your preparation. If you don't have a specific routine, consider developing one with the help of your coach or teammates.

What routine(s) do you work on during your practice sessions?

_____

_____

What is your routine before a game or match?

_____

_____

What is your routine during a game or match?

_____

_____

In what ways, if any, do these differ?

_____

_____

Perhaps you also have routines to help you recover after a game or practice, like icing your arm or having a favorite snack. List those here.

_____

_____

_____

game time mindful takeaway   Mindful athletes prepare their bodies and minds in practice and before and after games so they can be more successful *during* the actual game. They anticipate what might happen on the field so they can be ready for whatever might come up. Mental preparation allows you to create a positive mind-set so you can play your best, be more consistent, and remain more balanced and under control during the competition.

something more

The next time you're watching a collegiate or professional sporting event, try to arrive early and notice how the different athletes prepare and what types of routines they use. What did you notice that you could personally use the next time you get ready for a practice session or game? What things are they doing that you like? What, if anything, do you find a bit strange?

_____

_____

_____

_____

locker room activity: an informal mindfulness practice 19

Talking about attitude, Lleyton Hewitt, the youngest top-ranked male singles tennis player said, "Matches are won and lost so many times in the locker room."

In moments of adversity, it's often the player or team with the most poise and positive focused attitude that will prevail. Attitude and level of confidence play big roles in an athlete's ability to be resilient and perform at a high level. Even if you don't win the game, a positive attitude will allow you to bounce back more quickly from a disappointing loss or poor performance.

You may be thinking *How can I have a positive attitude and raise my level of confidence if I'm feeling beaten down after?* A lot of it has to do with the contents in your locker—your mental locker.

the mental locker

Your mind is a lot like a locker!

- ✓ Finding things in it can be difficult.

- ✓ It can hold a lot of different things.

- ✓ It can often get overstuffed.

- ✓ Sometimes you can get lost looking in it, and ruminate over things that happened or get overwhelmed by worries.

- ✓ Some of its contents are clean, new, and helpful (like the confident thought *I can get a hit against any pitcher*) while others are wet, smelly, and of no use (an anxious thought like *I always struggle playing away games*).

You can be in a hurry to change and quickly throw stuff into your locker or equipment bag. At other times, you're not rushing so you hang out by the lockers and chill.

Your mental locker is similar. Sometimes your mind is in such a rush with so many different thoughts that you may not realize you've been thinking and talking so negatively. Other times you may notice what you're thinking because you slow down and hang out with your mind. Once you begin to see how your thoughts impact your behavior and your performance, you can start to choose different, more confident and positive thoughts and attitudes.

take a look in your mental locker

So what's in your mental locker right now—thoughts about how tired or sore you are; judging thoughts about teammates, coaches, or opposing players; frustrated thoughts about lack of playing time; unconfident thoughts about how hard something is? List these thoughts here:

_____

_____

_____

_____

Just as items get forgotten about, lost, or dirty if your locker isn't cleaned out from time to time, your mind needs the same attention and care to its thoughts. You need to be aware of your negative thoughts because they influence your behavior and can lower your confidence and decrease your performance.

What items (negative thoughts) do you have that need to be cleaned out? You can look at what you wrote in your previous answer to help you.

_____

_____

_____

_____

For example, perhaps you're very hard on a teammate or yourself after a loss or poor performance and say unkind words. This then negatively impacts both of your confidence levels in the next game. Or maybe you're overconfident about playing a less talented team, thinking you'll win before you even take the field. This attitude might lead you to start being careless with the ball and make some silly mistakes during the game.

List some of the negative, nonhelpful thoughts in your mental locker here:

_____

_____

_____

_____

how to keep your mental locker clean

Just like having to clean out the junk from your locker during the season to make room for new equipment, you could benefit from replacing some negative attitudes and patterns of thoughts as well.

What new thoughts or attitudes could you add to your mental locker to help you or your teammates keep more positive, especially when things get tough?

For example, a runner who used to tell herself *I hate to train hard because my calves always hurt the next day* could instead think, *When I train hard, I know my muscles are getting stronger so I can be faster for the next race.*

List your positive thoughts here:

_____

_____

_____

_____

game time mindful takeaway   Be mindful of your mental locker, which can be filled with negative thoughts that need to be cleaned out. Begin to pay attention to how your thoughts and internal conversations (negative and positive) impact your behavior and your performance. Then you can start to choose different, more confident and positive thoughts and attitudes if you need to.

something more

creating your sports mantra

A *mantra* is a particular word or phrase you can repeat to help keep you focused when you start to feel the pressure of a sports situation. If you're a long distance or track runner and have a tendency to start thinking negatively when you get off to a slower start, a good mantra might be "Even strides even things up."

Think of a mantra you could silently repeat to help get you focused and calmer when you get stressed during your sport.

Write it here: _____

_____

_____

How do you feel when you read it?

_____

_____

What thoughts come to mind when you read it?

_____

_____

20 self-care for athletes

Speaking about the need for self-care, especially when life gets too intense, Olympic track and field gold medalist Sanya Richards-Ross said: "When I feel really stressed, the first thing I do is soak in a long bath. I love to read; it kind of quiets my mind."

The heart pumps blood to itself before the rest of the body's organs because it knows what it needs to do to survive. Like the heart, you need to care for yourself by filling yourself up with healthy things that support, promote, and nourish you every day. In order to be a good teammate, friend, family member, student, and more, you first have to be able to take care of yourself!

charting self-care

Self-care is a necessary part of human functioning. Like drinking water or eating food, if you don't put fuel in your self-care tank, you get to empty with nothing left to give yourself or others. Former NFL player Terrence Wheatley sums up self-care nicely: "Take one hour off the grid! No cell, no email, nothing. Also spoil yourself once a month."

To promote healthy self-care, there is a four-part plan called the *self-care gas tank*. Each quadrant offers suggestions on how to fill up your self-care gas tank, in different time intervals. The suggestions below are minimums. Obviously, the more healthy things you do to fill up your gas tank, the better.

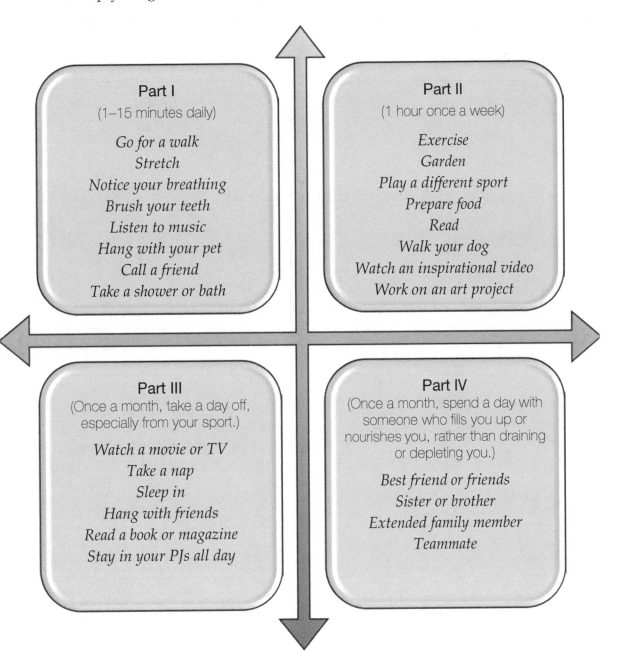

Part I
(1–15 minutes daily)

Go for a walk
Stretch
Notice your breathing
Brush your teeth
Listen to music
Hang with your pet
Call a friend
Take a shower or bath

Part II
(1 hour once a week)

Exercise
Garden
Play a different sport
Prepare food
Read
Walk your dog
Watch an inspirational video
Work on an art project

Part III
(Once a month, take a day off, especially from your sport.)

Watch a movie or TV
Take a nap
Sleep in
Hang with friends
Read a book or magazine
Stay in your PJs all day

Part IV
(Once a month, spend a day with someone who fills you up or nourishes you, rather than draining or depleting you.)

Best friend or friends
Sister or brother
Extended family member
Teammate

charting your self-care

For parts I–III, spend some time filling in all the things you can think of that you like to do. For part IV, think of the people you would like to spend time with. You can download a blank copy of this chart at http://www.newharbinger.com/40798.

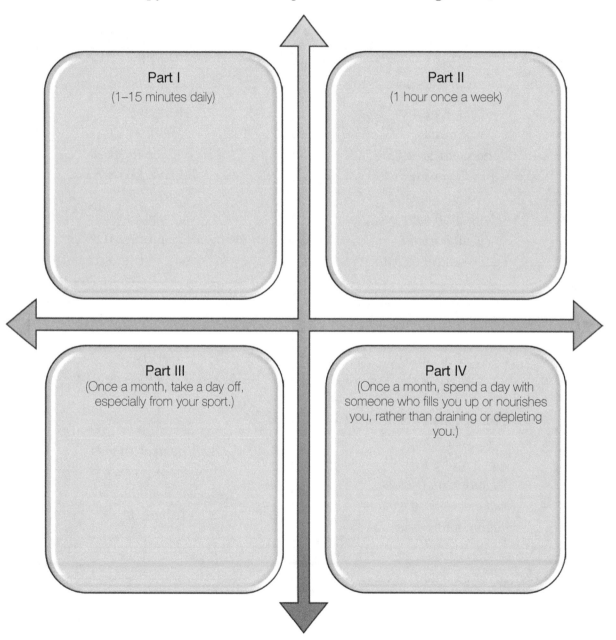

Part I
(1–15 minutes daily)

Part II
(1 hour once a week)

Part III
(Once a month, take a day off, especially from your sport.)

Part IV
(Once a month, spend a day with someone who fills you up or nourishes you, rather than draining or depleting you.)

game time mindful takeaway   The self-care gas tank is an important way to build a healthy reserve of good-for-you fuel to help you overcome daily life challenges and stressors. Resource yourself each day; fill up your self-care gas tank so you don't end up on empty.

something more

your current self-care gas tank

Where is your self-care gas tank right now—at full, half-full, nearly empty, or empty? In other words, how do your body and mind feel right now?

_____

_____

Now, circle a few of the top things you can do in each of the four quadrants—today, this week, and this month—to help fill up your self-care gas tank.

List a few of your top choices below:

Part I: I will do the following self-care activity today: _____ .

Part II: I will do the following self-care activity this week: _____ .

Part III: I will take a day off this month and do the following things: _____

_____ .

Part IV: I will spend the better part of a day with the following person who nourishes me this month: _____ .

Take a picture of your answers or put a note in your phone or calendar of the things you want to do today, this week, and this month. Get in touch with the person you want to hang out with for emotional nourishment.

After you have done a self-care activity today, this week, and this month, answer this question: after having filled up your self-care gas tank, how do you feel now?

_____

_____

_____

an attitude of gratitude 21

"An attitude of gratitude" is a phrase often used to encourage people to be grateful. It can be difficult to be grateful when you're stressed, losing a game, or when things just aren't going your way.

Answer the following questions before reading further:

What feeling(s) are you experiencing right now?

_____

_____

What are you thinking about right now?

_____

_____

What things have you been doing today before reading this?

_____

_____

What people, places, things, and situations in your life just don't seem to be going your way right now?

_____

_____

combat stress with gratitude: using the 5Gs

Gratitude is a way of expressing appreciation for what you have. Being grateful is the quality of being thankful. Most often when you're stressed, the last thing you want to think of is what you're grateful for. One of the best antidotes to combat stress is to have an attitude of gratitude.

Anytime you're stressed, you can quickly think of five things in your life that you're grateful for. If you have a hard time thinking of these, consider the people, places, things, and situations that you're thankful to have in your life.

List five things you are grateful for (aka your 5Gs).

1G: Right now, I am grateful for _____.

2G: Right now, I am grateful for _____.

3G: Right now, I am grateful for _____.

4G: Right now, I am grateful for _____.

5G: Right now, I am grateful for _____.

Now, answer the same questions you did above.

What feeling(s) are you experiencing right now?

_____

_____

What are you thinking about right now?

_____

_____

What people, places, things, and situations in your life just don't seem to be going your way right now?

_____

_____

_____

Are there any noticeable differences in how you feel or what you're thinking, or in your outlook about what isn't going right after thinking of your 5Gs?

_____

_____

_____

game time mindful takeaway   More often than not, just considering a few things you're grateful for can shift your mood and thinking away from being stressed or stuck in the negative to a less stressed and more positive outlook.

something more:
domains of gratitude

The grid below lists sixteen areas that people may be grateful for, including, for example, your basic needs, abilities, people, places, and things in your life that you can bring an attitude of gratitude to. Put a check next to each box that applies to you. For example, if you are mostly healthy, you can check the box labeled "Health." If you are grateful for something a coach (or teacher or mentor) does or has done for you, check the box labeled "Coaches/teachers/mentors."

Domains of Gratitude			
☐ Health	☐ Physical ability	☐ Place to live	☐ Clothes to wear
☐ Clean water to drink	☐ Clean air to breathe	☐ Food to eat	☐ Education
☐ Spirituality	☐ Job	☐ Money for things you want or need	☐ Ability to be involved in sports/clubs/hobbies
☐ Family	☐ Friends	☐ Coaches/ teachers/ mentors	☐ Nature

Looking at the areas you checked, reflect on how many domains of gratitude you marked as being areas you're grateful for. When you're stressed or having a difficult time, think of these areas. Remember, you can always revisit this grid to boost your attitude of gratitude.

finding your confident self

Retired American professional basketball player and member of the Women's Basketball Hall of Fame, Sheryl Swoopes, spoke to the importance of being confident: "If you do not believe yourself, no one else will."

Many athletes seek approval from others such as coaches, teammates, and fans to assess their value and ability, but confidence also needs to come from within. Your level of self-confidence is one thing that can set you apart from other athletes with equal physical ability.

self-confidence assessment

Self-confident people trust their abilities, qualities, decisions, power, and actions. Self-confidence comes from having a belief in yourself even when others might not. It isn't a made-up belief. It is recognizing and believing in your unique talents, strengths, and abilities. Focusing on these is going to help you when your inner critic is chiming in. Some questions to consider:

What physical abilities and skills do you use in athletics?

_____

_____

What qualities make you a good team member and team player?

_____

_____

What physical preparation have you put into playing your sport?

_____

_____

What mental time have you put into believing in your abilities and skills?

_____

_____

how to improve your
self-confidence in sports

In an article titled "7 Strategies to Help Your Athlete Be More Confident," Dr. Patrick J. Cohn, a leading sports psychologist, discussed these strategies: letting go of fear; playing freely instead of holding back; focusing on self—making no comparisons; playing for yourself, not others; playing functionally without trying to be perfect; being confident; and focusing on the process, not the results. The table below lists these strategies with examples that bring each to life. Reflect on each and then use the column on the right to write about how it applies to you.

Strategies	Example	How can you use this strategy?
1. Letting go of fear	*Colin fears making a mistake and letting his team down. This fear negatively affects his actual game play because he's often worried. Once Colin realizes worrying doesn't change the outcome and acknowledges just how much time he has put into practicing, he lets go of his fear. Colin also realizes that, like all athletes, he'll make mistakes, and that's part of playing sports.*	
2. Playing freely instead of holding back	*Shannon used to hold back in games because she didn't want to show off and was afraid of what others would think. Shannon has learned that her knowledge and belief in her skills allows her to freely use them during competition. She doesn't hold back any longer.*	
3. Focusing on self, not others, making no comparisons	*Mike used to focus on all the players on his team and opposing teams who played better than he did. He didn't focus on his own unique talents and value that he brings to the team. He's really good under pressure and is often sent in at difficult times. He now realizes that he, like everyone else, has his own value and is an asset to the team. He has stopped comparing himself to others as often.*	

Strategies	Example	How can you use this strategy?
4. Playing for yourself, not others	*Although Cindy played golf to please her parents, her true love was lacrosse. With the support of the lacrosse coach and her friends, she realized she needed to play for herself and not her parents. She talked to her parents and is now starting lacrosse next season.*	
5. Playing functionally without trying to be perfect	*Hamid tried to be perfect because that's what he was taught by some of his past coaches and trainers. His current coach realizes that mistakes are part and parcel of playing any sport and has provided a lot of support for Hamid. Hamid now recognizes that coaches, trainers, and parents must allow for mistakes.*	
6. Being confident	*Jamal has focused not only on his smooth swing in baseball but also on his skills in math, where he is one of the top students in his class. Developing as a whole person has helped Jamal build confidence.*	
7. Focusing on the process, not the results	*Heather was focused on being named MVP for the final game. After the game, she realized she didn't even know how her team had scored three goals. She had been playing on automatic pilot, which made it very difficult to play well, in the moment, and mindfully. Heather promised herself she would begin paying attention to the individual moments of the game itself.*	

game time mindful takeaway   The key to self-confidence is believing in yourself. Recognize your strengths, talents, and abilities as an athlete and as a person. To paraphrase Sheryl Swoopes, the more you believe in yourself, the more others will believe in you.

something more:
four keys to keeping self-confidence simple

Key 1: Practice

The best thing you can do to improve your confidence is to practice the sport.

Consider: Are you practicing your sport the way you would like to right now?

Key 2: Start With What's Easy

Start with something that comes easy for you in the sport you play and take in moments of success before going on to the most difficult aspects of your sport. Take in all moments of success!

Consider: Do you take in all the moments of your successes?

Key 3: Focus on Doing Your Best

Rather than *being* the best, focus on *doing* your best while you're playing. This includes being the best team member and team player you can.

Consider: Do you find you're doing your best as a team member and team player?

Key 4: Rightsize Your Fears of Failure

Fear limits your self-confidence. When you recognize your fear of failing, give yourself permission to make mistakes from time to time. You might have a bad day, game, play, and so on. The important thing is not to give up.

Consider: Do you give yourself permission to make mistakes?

After considering these four key areas of self-confidence, remember that each moment is a new opportunity to do something different.

athletic success: accepting failure and feedback 23

Michael Jordan reflects on his mistakes and failures: "I've missed more than nine thousand shots in my career. I've lost almost three hundred games. Twenty-six times I have been trusted to take the game-winning shot and missed. I've failed over and over again in my life—and that is why I succeed."

No one, not even Michael Jordan, is perfect! If Michael Jordan had focused on his mistakes and misses and couldn't let them go, he might not have become the winner of six NBA championships.

accepting failure leads to athletic success

It's important to be able to fail so that you can learn ways to take your game to the next level. Failing can provide you with valuable feedback on what you did wrong, ways to improve, and ways to do it differently next time. If you're open to failing, you're also open to taking risks, and it's during those risks that you can put it all on the line and possibly grow as a result. Failing is not an indication that you're not a good athlete or "less than" in some way.

What three things are you afraid of right now in the sport(s) you play?

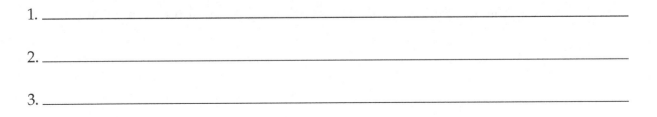

1. _____

2. _____

3. _____

What things are you *not* trying in the sport(s) you play because you're afraid of failure?

_____

_____

_____

take in feedback with the 3Cs

Offered by someone who has your best interest at heart, feedback helps you improve and succeed as an athlete even when it's hard to hear. The 3Cs can help you better accept feedback.

be centered

Take a mindful moment or pause. On your next in-breath, notice where you bring air in: through your nose or mouth? On your out-breath, notice where you send air out: through your nose or mouth? This automatically will calm you down and center you, which will allow you to listen to the feedback.

be curious

Keep an open mind about what is being said to you. Assume that this person wants you to improve in some way. Consider how you can be curious about what is being said and open to the possibility that this feedback might help you in some way.

be compassionate

Hearing feedback, even though someone is trying to be helpful, can still sting. Can you support yourself like you would your best friend? Be compassionate for the part of you that might be hurt. Be compassionate for those who are providing feedback if they are well intended. They are taking a risk in sharing their feedback with you. You could respond harshly to them.

game time mindful takeaway   The next time you receive feedback, use the 3Cs to be centered, curious, and compassionate. Learning to fail and having the ability to take in feedback are two keys to becoming a successful athlete.

something more:
the 3Cs in action

Reflect on the last time you received feedback from a person who was trying to help you, and answer the following:

What was the feedback you received?

_____

_____

_____

Who was providing you with the feedback?

_____

How did you respond to this person?

_____

_____

How could you have centered yourself?

_____

_____

_____

How could you have been curious with the feedback you received?

_____

_____

_____

How could you have been compassionate toward yourself and the person who provided the feedback?

_____

_____

_____

thoughts impact performance 24

Major League Baseball All-Star shortstop Francisco Lindor said, "If you bring negative thoughts to your life it can affect your game."

There are many factors that can impact an athlete's performance—skill set, amount of practice and preparation, experience, hydration and diet, physical stamina, fitness, or even the weather. One thing, however, that many athletes don't focus on is how their thoughts impact how they'll perform in the future. Many athletes get upset or frustrated when something doesn't go their way, especially when they make a mistake during a game or competition, and this can cause them to make another slipup. There's a helpful way to not let the negative thoughts that can arise during our mistakes get the better of us, and that's using a tool called mistake rituals.

mental mistake rituals

How do you deal with a poor performance event? All-Star caliber players use a sports psychology tool called mistake rituals to help them move past a blunder or error. A teammate or coach might tell you to just forget about a poor play or error, but it's not always easy to do so. If you've ever had trouble moving past a mistake, you can mentally and physically wipe it away. The idea is to link up the negative thoughts about making the mistake with thoughts about washing it away. For example, if you play your sport on ice, you could use the image of a Zamboni plowing over your mistake, leaving you a smooth surface on which to make your next play. If your sport is played in the water, you could use the image of a pool filter washing away your past mistake. If you are on an outside field, the image of a hose or sprinkler could be used to help rinse the error away.

Using your mind to wipe away a mistake the moment after it is made helps you reset to be ready for the next play. This helps you focus on the next moment during the game or competition, not a mistake you made in the past. You can always go back later to evaluate your full performance, but it's best to wait until your competition is over so you don't cloud your mind with negative thoughts.

physical mistake rituals

Sometimes you just need a brief physical move that will quickly help you disconnect from having made a poor play or error. Physical mistake rituals are motions that athletes make, usually with their fingers, hands, or feet, to signify disconnecting or separating from and then moving past a performance mistake. It doesn't undo the error, but it does allow you to stop the negative thoughts that arise from it. You could adopt the same kinds of gestures you might use for a game of charades. Some motions you can make include wiping away, cutting, hammering, flushing, raking, blowing, kicking, pushing, or throwing.

For example, some baseball players rake and smooth the dirt with their cleats after making an error. Soccer players sometimes stamp their cleats on the ground in an attempt to clean the mud or grass out of their spikes. Lacrosse or field hockey players might turn over and repeatedly shake their sticks as a signal of letting go of a bad shot. Wrestlers, gymnasts, or cheerleaders could take a towel or shirt, or use their socks or hands, and wipe the mat or their forehead as a sign of wiping away the mistake.

List some of the types of mistakes or errors that you or your teammates are more prone to making in your sport.

_____

_____

_____

_____

Now list at least one mistake ritual you could use for each type of error or poor play.

_____

_____

_____

_____

game time mindful takeaway   The next time you make a mistake during a game or competition, remember to use a mistake ritual to help you move past the negative thinking that may impact your performance.

something more

US Olympic gold medalist Missy Franklin said, "If I'm ever really stressed out or nervous before a race, I start to think about the things that aren't going to change in my life, regardless of what the impact of that race is."

Like Missy Franklin, when you think about the things in your life that are more constant or consistent—support from your teammates, family, and friends or the love from a pet—you can feel a bit more grounded and calmer. What are some things in your life that aren't going to change regardless of the outcome of your next game, the result of the race, or your performance? List them here:

_____

_____

_____

_____

_____

The next time you are feeling stressed out before a game or competition, think about some of the things on this list.

Lynn Jennings, one of the best American female long-distance runners of all time, said, "Mental will is a muscle that needs exercise, just like muscles of the body."

Mentally tough athletes have a stronger ability to focus, rebound from failure, handle pressure, and persist in the face of adversity. In other words, they are resilient and perform at a higher level. Mental toughness is a skill you can develop and increase.

the 4 Cs of mental toughness: control, commitment, challenge, and confidence

Control means the extent to which athletes feel in control of their lives, their circumstances, and their emotions. How much control do you feel right now as an athlete?

_____

Commitment describes the degree to which athletes are prepared to set goals for what they want and how hard they work to deliver on what they set out to do. How committed are you to your goals?

_____

Challenge illustrates how athletes will push their limits, embrace change, and accept risk. Do you see adversity as an opportunity or a threat?

_____

Confidence is an internal belief in your own sports abilities and how you handle conflicts and challenges on and off the field. How confident are you in your sports abilities?

_____

exercising your mental will

On a scale of 1 to 10 (10 being the highest in mental toughness), how would you rate your current level of

Control   _____

Commitment   _____

Challenge   _____

Confidence   _____

Any of the components of mental toughness can be enhanced. Choose one of the 4 Cs you wish to increase at this moment and write about it here.

_____

_____

_____

enhancing mental toughness with positive self-talk

Positive self-talk uses short, memorable, present-based, positively worded messages for keeping your mind focused on the good. Imagine encouraging a friend during a difficult time. Those kind, optimistic words are the ones you might use with your own positive self-talk.

While the majority of positive self-talk takes place in silence in your head, it can be both instructional ("Keep focused on the ball") and motivational ("I got this").

Below is a list of messages that athletes often use when talking to themselves. Place a *P* next to those that are positive self-talk and an *N* next to those that are more negative or neutral self-talk.

_____   I'll get the next one.

_____   I should've made that play.

_____   Make solid contact.

_____   Take a deep breath.

_____   Reach.

_____   Lean forward.

_____   I give up.

_____   Stay alert.

_____   I'm not good enough.

_____   I can do this.

> game time mindful takeaway   Remember, the key to using positive self-talk is to use words that are short, memorable, optimistic, and based in the present. Mentally tough athletes make good choices about what they choose to think and use as self-talk.

something more

your positive self-talk statements

All-Star pitcher Andrew Miller said, "Confidence is this game. That's what it's all about." Increasing confidence will increase your overall mental toughness. In order to be more resilient, come up with three or four of your own positive self-talk phrases that you can use during a game or competition. Remember to keep them short, positive, easy to remember, and based in the present. List your positive self-talk phrases here.

_____

_____

_____

_____

_____

mental car wash 26

Danica Patrick, professional stock-car racer, said, "I think you have to feel comfortable with your car. You have to go into turn one, every lap, with confidence. You have to be sure of yourself and your equipment."

If you drove a clean car, with all the filth washed away by a car wash, you might feel that it runs much more smoothly. Perhaps you would also have more confidence in your driving since you would be able to more clearly see out of your windows.

If you've played outdoor sports, you've likely had a game or practice in nasty weather—hard rain, wind, ice-cold temps, or scorching high heat. Perhaps you've had an exhausting practice session and wound up dirty or drenched in sweat, the equivalent of that filthy car. Now, think of how you felt after you had a hot shower and the chance to chill and rest. You probably felt more refreshed and relaxed. You would also likely be better ready and have more energy to compete in your next game.

what is a mental car wash?

Your mind, like a car, can get full of grime too. Particularly after a tough loss, intense practice session, or multiday tournament, your mind can get crammed full of stressful, negative, judgmental, or anxious thoughts. Maybe you're mentally beating yourself up because you didn't perform as you would've liked. Or maybe you had the game of your life and are wondering how you'll ever be able to do that again. These negative mental thoughts can erode your confidence and level of comfort in your sport.

Thoughts like "I'm awful!" "I played like crap," "I hate my coach," and "We always lose to that team" clog up your mind and tend to leave a lasting negative impression like dead bugs plastered on the windshield after a long drive. They make it hard to see clearly and need to be wiped off. In certain instances, it can be helpful to reflect on a poor performance or tough loss to see what you might've learned about yourself and your level of resilience. Sometimes, though, you just need to be able to wash away a poor performance or disappointing loss and forget about it.

taking a mental car wash:
the five-step process

Step 1. Bring to mind the distressing emotions and thoughts you felt or are still feeling about your performance. Imagine you're watching that game or practice on a movie screen and do your best to see yourself there.

Step 2. Take a few deep breaths, sending the energy of your breath to any areas of discomfort in your body. You can even just breathe in and send your breath down through your whole body and through the soles of your feet and into the ground.

Step 3. Picture yourself walking through the car wash while it's in full operation. See and feel the brushes, water, and soap washing off your stresses, anxieties, worries, anger, frustrations—whatever you experienced from the tough event.

Step 4. Watch as the residue from your distressing thoughts and unpleasant emotions of your game or practice session start to get washed off and rinsed down the floor drains.

Step 5. Imagine that you're now going through the warmth of the dryers.

Describe how you feel and your level of confidence after having given yourself a mental car wash.

_____

_____

_____

_____

_____

What is still stuck on you?

_____

_____

_____

_____

What feels better?

_____

_____

_____

_____

game time mindful takeaway   Just like taking a warm, relaxing shower after a hard practice, game, or competition, use the five steps of a mental car wash to help alleviate any mental or emotional stresses, anxieties, or worries from the day.

something more

recharge your batteries

Chilling out after a tough game, poor performance, or extra-hard practice session can be quite helpful. Look at the list below and check off those things you have done before to recharge your batteries.

☐ Browse the Internet   ☐ Talk on the phone or FaceTime

☐ Chat with friends on social media   ☐ Watch a movie or TV

☐ Go out with friends   ☐ Spend time with a pet or family

☐ Play video games   ☐ Eat at a restaurant

☐ Read   ☐ Take a walk or relax outside

☐ Shop   ☐ Listen to or play music

☐ Sleep   ☐ Mental car wash

☐ Other: _____

High-performing athletes usually deal with a lot of stress on and off the field. One of the most helpful things you can do for your body and mind is to find healthy ways to relax. The mental car wash is a good way to unwind, but it's certainly not the only way to chill. Look at the list above again, and make sure to incorporate at least one or two other items into your routine.

controlling the controllables

Major League Baseball pitcher Trevor Bauer summed up nicely what it means to stay within yourself and control what is in your power to control: "I don't worry about the things I can't control. I can control my preparation and my attitude on the mound and how I go about attacking. If I give in—I can control that. I can't control the results, who I face, or when I pitch."

The irony here is that one of the things mindfulness allows athletes to experience is the feeling that they're more in control of their lives, both on and off the field, yet so many things are beyond our control. The challenge is knowing and focusing on those things you can control.

focus on the controllables

Your attitude and how you respond to situations and events are very much in your control. Stress, worry, and anxiety will increase when we get caught up in thinking we can control those things that are really out of our control.

Below is a list of things that can impact the outcome of a game or competition. Circle those things over which you have control.

your coach	winning and losing
your teammate's performance	your equipment
your effort	the people in the stands
the weather	the official or referee's decisions
the other team or competitors	your hydration and diet
your playing surface	luck
your attitude	the schedule
scoring a goal or getting a hit	the traffic or bus ride

Now look back at that list. What surprised you about this exercise?

_____

_____

_____

game time mindful takeaway   You cannot control what happens to you or around you, but you can control your attitude and how you choose to respond. Being mindful will help recognize what you can and cannot control.

something more

Controlling the controllables can apply to your life outside of sports and competition. Choose one of these categories—school, your friends, your family, or your neighbors—and list three things you can control and three things you cannot.

Category: _____

Can control

1. _____

2. _____

3. _____

Can't control

1. _____

2. _____

3. _____

28 tracking sports performance

Whether on your smartphone, wall, school planner, or elsewhere, charting can be instructive, informational, or sometimes even motivational. It's a great tool to help you get and stay organized. Charting information can also help you become more aware of events that are happening in your life, and increasing your awareness is a key skill in helping you enhance athletic performance while reducing stress and worry.

peak performance sporting event chart

Think back on some of your recent athletic experiences. Use the chart below (or download a blank chart at http://www.newharbinger.com/40798) to map out some of those times in the last week or two when you were performing very well or at your peak. There are five columns for you to consider.

Strong performance event	How did your body feel? What physical sensations did you notice?	What feelings and/or emotions occurred?	What thoughts occurred?	What are you feeling and thinking now?
Example: Scored a goal	I felt energized. My heart was racing.	I felt excited and pumped. I was proud of my goal.	I can't believe how I got past that defender.	I'm feeling pretty good. I think I am a solid player.

Strong performance event	How did your body feel? What physical sensations did you notice?	What feelings and/or emotions occurred?	What thoughts occurred?	What are you feeling and thinking now?

Look back at some of your entries on this chart. Do you see any patterns of thoughts, feelings, or bodily sensations? What else do you notice from these peak sporting experiences?

_____

_____

_____

Major League Baseball manager Terry Francona perfectly summed up why it is also important to pay attention to your sports performance when things are not going your way. "So much of our season is how you deal with frustration. That defines your season." It's a great way to review your progress. Let's look now at those times when you were not at your best.

nonpeak performance sporting event chart

Weak performance event	How did your body feel? What physical sensations did you notice?	What feelings and/or emotions occurred?	What thoughts occurred?	What are you feeling and thinking now?
Example: Got called for a penalty	My legs felt heavy. My throat felt tight and hard to swallow.	I was upset and angry at the ref.	I hate the ref. The other player should have been called for it too.	I shouldn't have lost my cool. I feel a bit embarrassed. I'll do better next game.

Weak performance event	How did your body feel? What physical sensations did you notice?	What feelings and/or emotions occurred?	What thoughts occurred?	What are you feeling and thinking now?

Look back at some of your entries into this chart. Do you see any patterns of thoughts, feelings, or bodily sensations?

_____

_____

_____

_____

_____

How were your responses different from the Peak Performance Sporting Event Chart?

_____

_____

_____

_____

_____

game time mindful takeaway   Pay attention to those times when you are in the zone and performing at your peak state, as well as those times when you're struggling to perform well. Noticing your thoughts, feelings, and bodily sensations during these moments of activity and later in reflection can help you gain insight into how your mind and body work best. You can then see what triggers your optimal behavior and actions and use that information to help you during your next sports performance.

something more

You can use peak and nonpeak charts for any different types of activities, including your schoolwork. Select one or two different nonsports activities or events, and use these charts to shed light on what made you perform at a higher level and perhaps what made your performance less than ideal.

Peak event	How did your body feel? What physical sensations did you notice?	What feelings and/or emotions occurred?	What thoughts occurred?	What are you feeling and thinking now?

Nonpeak event	How did your body feel? What physical sensations did you notice?	What feelings and/or emotions occurred?	What thoughts occurred?	What are you feeling and thinking now?

managing and breaking through pain 29

"As an athlete, you are literally programmed to endure a specific amount of pain." Abby Wambach, US Olympic soccer gold medalist and FIFA World Player of the Year understands something about physical pain; she was known for scoring many of her goals with driving headers.

Most athletes experience some sort of aches and pains during the season. Being a mindful athlete enables you to be more aware of and better cope with uncomfortable feelings in your body, like physical pain. Deep awareness of discomfort, soreness, or pain in your body allows you to properly address it.

how to manage and break through pain

As a student athlete, you've likely experienced pain and perhaps even an injury. Pain cannot be avoided, but injuries can sometimes be lessened, the more you listen to your body and the pain. Every athlete's body responds to pain differently, so it's important to learn how to be more aware of pain and to best manage it.

For an athlete, there's a difference between experiencing pain and sustaining an injury. Physical pain is an uncomfortable awareness in your body that alerts you when something may be wrong and needs your attention. Pushing through physical pain if you aren't fully aware of your body's sensations can sometimes lead to greater pain and injury. Injury is an instance of harm or damage to the body. There are different levels of pain, of course, and degrees of injury: some minor like a small cut, scrape, or soft bruise, and others more impactful, like an ankle sprain or hamstring strain, that need time to heal. The key is to bring mindful attention to your body and not let the pain overwhelm you.

being comfortable with the uncomfortable: noticing the sensations of pain

Mindfulness allows us to be comfortable with the uncomfortable. That doesn't mean you're delighted to have pain in your back, muscle soreness in your legs, or an injury; it just means you don't let it get the best of you. Let's notice some of the different sensations that come with pain or discomfort.

- Get an ice cube (or two) and hold it in the palm of your exposed hand.

- Notice the physical sensations in your hand, fingers, and other parts of your body.

- Pay attention to the thoughts that are arising about holding the ice cube.

- Now notice what feelings, if any, are coming up for you as you hold the ice cube.

- Take a few deep breaths and again feel the sensations of the ice cube in your hand, and then just dispose of the ice cube.

What did you notice about your body and perception of pain or discomfort as you held the ice cube?

_____

_____

_____

game time mindful takeaway   The experience of pain is just that, an experience, a feeling in your body. Yes, it can be rather uncomfortable, rather painful. The key is to notice the actual sensations of the pain and how those may change over time. In this way, you're able to better cope with the feeling of pain or discomfort rather than trying to avoid it.

something more

tuning in to your breath while in pain

This book has highlighted the importance of using your breath for helping you calm your mind and relax an anxious, nervous, or overwhelmed body. Your breath can also aid in your ability to better cope with pain, muscle soreness, and even injury.

First, quickly scan your body to notice any areas that seem to be sore, or have some pain or discomfort. Picture that area of your body (you can gently touch or rub it, if you wish). Take a few deep breaths, and imagine that as you breathe you are sending the energy and oxygen from your breath to and through that area of discomfort for the next few moments. How does that area feel now?

_____

_____

_____

30 stress equals pain times blocking: S=PxB

Chrissie Wellington, three-time Ironman World Championship triathlon winner, knows a thing or two about enduring, breaking through, and managing pain: "I know I can reach those limits, those thresholds, push beyond them and come out the other side. Expect it will be painful and have faith in yourself that you will overcome those dark times."

You are going to experience physical and emotional pain; it is part of the human condition. How you manage and handle the pain will affect how stressed you are by it.

blocking your pain makes your stress worse

Pain is inevitable in life; stress is optional! Accept pain, both physical and emotional.

Your overall stress level in any painful moment can be greatly diminished depending on how you manage it, or what is called *blocking* in this activity. Many things people do don't fix the pain, but instead put a Band-Aid on it, prolong it, make it worse, or cause an entirely new set of problems. Blocking includes any actions and behaviors that aren't actually helping you manage your pain in a productive and positive way.

Below is a list of common blocking behaviors. Circle any of these behaviors that you engage in when you experience physical or emotional pain:

resisting the problem

avoiding the problem

pushing the problem away

denying that the problem exists

ignoring the pain it causes

feeling guilty about it

obsessing about it

ruminating about it

judging yourself

telling yourself you should have, could have, or would have done something different

feeling guilty about it

engaging in unhelpful or harmful coping behaviors (such as cutting or restricting your food)

Now you can see how you block your pain. Doing this is not meant to make you feel bad, or to have you start mentally beating yourself up. Many people block their pain because they don't have more productive ways to positively cope with it. You can use the previous activities in this book as ways to positively manage painful life events.

At any time, you can choose to reduce any of the blocking behaviors (unhelpful and harmful coping behaviors) you marked.

plotting your pain with the equation S=PxB

Go through the example below to learn how Jeff reduced his stress by plotting his pain and blocking using the equation S=PxB.

1. Describe the person, place, thing, or situation causing you pain.

    Jeff twisted his ankle last week playing football. He wasn't able to play all last week and has been restricted from playing for another week.

2. What kind of pain are you experiencing?

    Jeff is in a lot of physical pain. His ankle hurts even when he isn't walking on it. It's difficult to get around at home and at school.

3. How much pain are you in from 0 units (no pain) to 100 units (the worst pain you could ever imagine)?

    Jeff reports 100 units of pain.

4. What blocking behaviors are you engaging in? Refer to the list on the previous page to help you. Assign 10 units of blocking to each behavior.

    After going through the list above, Jeff realizes (1) he's pushing the problem away; (2) he isn't taking his ibuprofen; (3) he isn't icing his ankle the way the doctor suggested; (4) he's blaming himself for going in for that last tackle; (5) he thinks that if he hadn't, he would have prevented his ankle pain; (6) he's been isolating himself from his teammates; (7) he didn't go to the game last week even though he was supposed to; and (8) he isn't doing the rehab his coach recommended.

5. How much are you blocking, from 0 units (no blocking) to 100 units (a high amount of blocking)?

Jeff determines that he has 80 units of blocking.

Jeff charts his pain and blocking and connects the two to see how stressed he is.

Jeff realizes he currently is experiencing 8,000 units of stress.

BEFORE

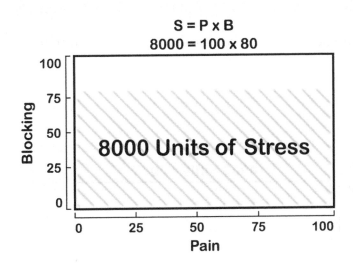

Now that Jeff has learned what blocking is and has been able to identify the blocking behaviors he's using, he can make some changes, gain some control over his problem, and reduce his stress.

6. Even if the pain stayed the same number, what blocking behaviors could you change, reduce, or eliminate?

Jeff decides that (1) he'll go to the game this coming Friday; (2) he'll increase his icing; (3) he'll go to the movies with friends; (4) he'll start doing some of the rehab his coach suggested. He doesn't change all his blocking behaviors, but he improves some of them.

7. Now how much are you blocking, from 0 units (no blocking) to 100 units (a high amount of blocking)?

Jeff is still blocking at 40 units, but this is down a lot from his 80 units.

Now Jeff plots the new blocking amount and sees how much he can change his stress.

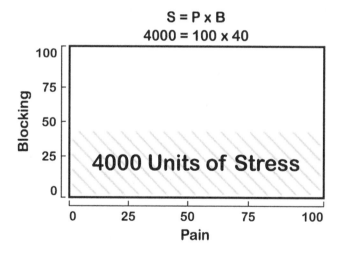

AFTER

S = P x B
4000 = 100 x 40

Jeff was able to reduce his overall stress by half just by changing a few of his blocking behaviors. Changing this greatly impacted his overall mood, functioning, and healing.

game time mindful takeaway   The more people attach to, pull toward, push away, or avoid the person, place, thing, or situation, the more they increase their stress and suffering. You can reduce your stress by reducing how you block painful life moments.

something more:
you have some control over your stress

You can reduce your stress and increase your sense of power, agency, and control by changing how you block painful moments. Think of something that is causing you physical or emotional pain right now.

1. Describe the person, place, thing, or situation causing you pain.

   _____

   _____

   _____

2. What kind of pain are you experiencing?

   _____

   _____

3. How much pain are you in, from 0 units (no pain) to 100 units (the worst pain you could ever imagine)?

_____

4. What blocking behaviors are you engaging in? Refer to the list earlier in this activity to help you. Assign 10 units of blocking to each behavior.

_____

_____

_____

_____

_____

5. How much are you blocking, from 0 units (no blocking) to 100 units (a high amount of blocking)?

_____

Use this chart to plot how stressed you are. At http://www.newharbinger.com /40798, you can download a blank version.

BEFORE

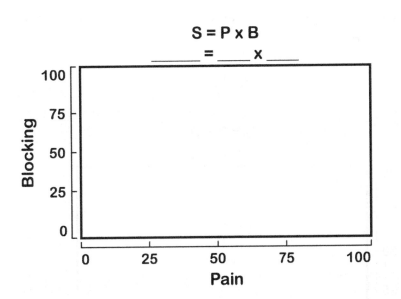

6. Even if the pain stayed the same number, what blocking behaviors could you change, reduce, or eliminate?

_____

_____

_____

_____

_____

7. Now how much are you blocking, from 0 units (no blocking) to 100 units (a high amount of blocking)?

_____

Use this blank chart to plot how stressed you are after you change some of your blocking behaviors.

AFTER

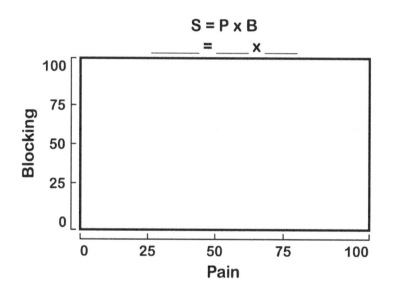

Compare the two diagrams and see how you can change your stress level by changing, reducing, or eliminating some or all of your blocking behaviors.

visualizing your performance 31

Olympic soccer gold medalist and FIFA Women's World Cup champion Alex Morgan said, "To perform at a high level I get myself in the right mind-set and do mental visualization."

Mental visualization, as Alex Morgan calls it, is also often called mental rehearsal, guided imagery, or just imagery. Athletes can use mental visualization in many ways, such as enhancing motivation, improving concentration, building confidence, controlling emotions, and coping with pain or injury, to help in practicing a particular sports skill. It's a process of picturing in your mind what you want to have happen in the future. It creates a state of confidence in your body and a mind-set as if you're experiencing the actual event. In fact, the neurons in the brain that fire if you are, for example, hitting a golf ball or swimming, are the same ones that fire if you're just thinking about hitting a golf ball or swimming. Our minds don't know the difference between what we vividly imagine and what is actually real.

the six steps to mental visualization

The keys for using visualization effectively are using as much detail as possible and controlling your images so that you can manipulate them. You also want to consider the point of view of your visualization. Are you watching yourself perform the action as if from a distance outside looking in (like watching yourself on a movie screen) or are you visualizing yourself as if you are in the movie actually taking the actions?

Step 1. Find a quiet place when first starting. As you get more comfortable using visualization, you might want to practice in the same settings as your particular sport.

Step 2. Take a few deep breaths to help relax you.

Step 3. Picture all the details as vividly as possible (involving all your senses) of what you desire to have happen, while also controlling the images to do what you want.

Step 4. Make sure to imagine specific situations you might actually experience during a game or competition.

Step 5. Like self-talk, focus on positive outcomes where you're successfully doing what you want to do.

Step 6. Act as though your goal of what you have visualized has already happened.

Choose something specific to your sport that you wish to visualize and write it down here. Perhaps you want to imagine yourself scoring a goal, making a basket, or finishing first in a race.

Now go through each of the six steps and visualize yourself having done what you wrote down.

What did you notice while doing this exercise?

_____

_____

_____

How might you actually use mental visualization in your chosen sport?

_____

_____

_____

game time mindful takeaway   Remember to make your visualization as vivid as possible, using all your senses, and to work at trying to control the image to do exactly what you wish it to do. Act as though the outcome you visualized has already happened.

something more

mindfully managing wins and losses

You can visualize your performance to mindfully manage wins and losses. Hall of Famer Ernie Banks said, "The only way to prove that you're a good sport is to lose." Most athletes, and coaches for that matter, don't like to lose. However, it's important to show good sportsmanship and shake hands or congratulate the winner. This is certainly not always easy to do so, especially when we lose a very tough game or competition or have had what we felt was a poor performance.

First, visualize yourself after losing a game, race, or competition. Imagine yourself responding to the loss in a fair and professional way, showing yourself to be a good sport.

Next, visualize yourself after winning a game, race, or competition.

What differences did you notice between losing with good sportsmanship and winning?

_____

_____

_____

the positive and nurturing coach 32

US Olympic gold medalist Simone Biles acknowledges how important it is to be a positive and nurturing coach: "I believe that if you are in a good place mentally and emotionally, the confidence will come through."

We've already covered the benefits of managing your internal conversations with the locker room and car wash activities, as well as using positive self-talk to help build confidence and overall mental toughness. The idea behind the Positive and Nurturing Coach is to take this to the next level so you can be your own motivational and inspirational voice.

mantras make room for the positive and nurturing coach

Mantras are words or phrases that you repeat aloud or think over and over. They become a part of who you are as an athlete and a person. Many professional and Olympic athletes use mantras in their quest to perform at a higher level. Some mantras that athletes use are: "I got this." "Because I can." "Next one." "Every step gets me closer to my goal." "It's all part of the process."

The benefits of mantras are many:

- ✓ lowering cortisol levels, reducing stress
- ✓ quieting and calming the mind
- ✓ enhancing endurance and performance
- ✓ reducing perception of effort during physical exertion
- ✓ possibly lessening your need for self-judgment
- ✓ strengthening neural pathways in your brain

Here are some things to consider when using mantras:

- Create several mantras to use in different situations.

- Keep them short and positive.

- Practice your mantra before actual unease occurs in your sporting event.

- Picture new powerful neural pathways and connections forming in your brain.

Now it's your turn. Create two or three mantras you can use when you face any adversity or challenge on and off the athletic field. Remember, you can use the mantra that you came up with earlier in this book.

_____

_____

_____

_____

_____

game time mindful takeaway   Like high-achieving athletes, you too can use mantras to create a positive and nurturing coach within. Make sure your words or phrases are positive, short, and meaningful to you, and practice them before the actual sporting event.

something more

I am ...

The words you use to describe yourself are powerful and creative. They can help you behave and act differently. Choose three words and write them down below to represent who you want to be on the practice field and during your game or athletic competition; for example, focused, agile, relentless, powerful, fast.

I am _____

I am _____

I am _____

Repear these mantras often, especially at night before falling asleep and in the morning when you wake up.

Now that you have your mantras and three words that describe who you want to be when you're playing sports, you're well on your way to being a positive and nurturing coach to yourself—and a mindful student athlete.

Gina M. Biegel, MA, LMFT, is a psychotherapist, researcher, speaker, and author in the San Francisco Bay Area who specializes in mindfulness-based work with adolescents. She is the founder of Stressed Teens, which has been offering mindfulness-based stress reduction for teens (MBSR-T) to adolescents, families, schools, professionals, and the community for over a decade. She created MBSR-T to help teens in a large HMO's outpatient department of child and adolescent psychiatry who were not receiving relief or amelioration of their physical and psychological symptoms with the use of a multitude of other evidence-based practices. An expert and pioneer in bringing mindfulness-based approaches to youth, she is the author of *Be Mindful and Stress Less*, *The Stress Reduction Workbook for Teens* (first and second edition), and the *Be Mindful Card Deck for Teens*. She also has a mindfulness practice audio CD, *Mindfulness for Teens*, to complement the MBSR-T program. She provides intensive ten-week online trainings worldwide and works with teens and families individually and in groups. Her work has been featured on *The Today Show* and *CNN*, and in *Reuters*, *The New York Times*, and *Tricycle*. For more information, visit her website at www.stressedteens.com.

Todd H. Corbin, CPC, is a former multisport student athlete and youth baseball coach, longtime avid runner and sports enthusiast, mindfulness teacher, professional speaker, certified parenting coach, and parent to two teen athletes. Mistakenly labeled as learning disabled in first grade left Todd with very low self-esteem and many social and emotional scars. As a result, he turned his attention to helping others find ways to use mindful awareness to build self-confidence and resilience, overcome stress and anxiety, and enhance performance. He spent twenty-one years in higher education publishing and was an instructor at Lakeland Community College in Ohio for twelve years, teaching courses in stress management, peak performance, communication skills, mindfulness, and meditation.

Todd's overall knowledge of mindfulness, stress management, and meditation is extensive. He has been practicing and teaching mindfulness since 1994, integrating the most current research in neuroscience and optimal performance. He received formal training in mindfulness from many of the leading experts and programs in the field. Todd also received personal training in meditation and overall well-being directly from best-selling authors Deepak Chopra and Neale Donald Walsch which led to the creation of a mindfulness-based stress relief curriculum for children/teens taught for three years at The Chopra Center for Wellbeing in Carlsbad, CA. For more information on Todd, visit his website at www.toddcorbin.com.

Real change *is* possible

For more than forty-five years, New Harbinger has published proven-effective self-help books and pioneering workbooks to help readers of all ages and backgrounds improve mental health and well-being, and achieve lasting personal growth. In addition, our spirituality books offer profound guidance for deepening awareness and cultivating healing, self-discovery, and fulfillment.

Founded by psychologist Matthew McKay and Patrick Fanning, New Harbinger is proud to be an independent, employee-owned company. Our books reflect our core values of integrity, innovation, commitment, sustainability, compassion, and trust. Written by leaders in the field and recommended by therapists worldwide, New Harbinger books are practical, accessible, and provide real tools for real change.

newharbingerpublications

More ⏱Instant Help Books for Teens

An Imprint of New Harbinger Publications

THE INSOMNIA WORKBOOK FOR TEENS

Skills to Help You Stop Stressing & Start Sleeping Better

978-1684031245 / US $17.95

EATING MINDFULLY FOR TEENS

A Workbook to Help You Make Healthy Choices, End Emotional Eating & Feel Great

978-1684030033 / US $16.95

THE GRIT GUIDE FOR TEENS

A Workbook to Help You Build Perseverance, Self-Control & a Growth Mindset

978-1626258563 / US $16.95

THE STRESS REDUCTION WORKBOOK FOR TEENS, SECOND EDITION

Mindfulness Skills to Help You Deal with Stress

978-1684030187 / US $16.95

THE ANXIETY WORKBOOK FOR TEENS

Activities to Help You Deal with Anxiety & Worry

978-1572246034 / US $15.95

COPING WITH CLIQUES

A Workbook to Help Girls Deal with Gossip, Put-Downs, Bullying & Other Mean Behavior

978-1572246133 / US $16.95

🌱 **newharbingerpublications**
1-800-748-6273 / newharbinger.com

(VISA, MC, AMEX / prices subject to change without notice)

Follow Us 🇫 🐦 📷 📌

Register your **new harbinger** titles for additional benefits!

When you register your **new harbinger** title—purchased in any format, from any source—you get access to benefits like the following:

- Downloadable accessories like printable worksheets and extra content

- Instructional videos and audio files

- Information about updates, corrections, and new editions

Not every title has accessories, but we're adding new material all the time.

Access free accessories in 3 easy steps:

1. Sign in at NewHarbinger.com (or **register** to create an account).

2. Click on **register a book**. Search for your title and click the **register** button when it appears.

3. Click on the **book cover or title** to go to its details page. Click on **accessories** to view and access files.

That's all there is to it!

If you need help, visit:

NewHarbinger.com/accessories

new harbinger
CELEBRATING
40 YEARS